FEED

THE CAMELS

McDougal & Associates
Servants of Christ and stewards of the mysteries of God

FEED

THE CAMELS

SERVING YOUR DESTINY
THROUGH THE UNIMPORTANT
THINGS OF LIFE

BY

ANDRÉ VAN ZYL

Published by:

McDougal & Associates
P.O. Box 194
Greenwell Springs, LA 70739-0194
www.thepublishedword.com

McDougal & Associates is dedicated to the spreading of the Gospel of Jesus Christ to as many people as possible in the shortest time possible.

ISBN 13: 978-0-9777053-3-7
ISBN 10: 0-9777053-3-1
Printed in the United States of America
For Worldwide Distribution

DEDICATION

To Naomi, my wife, and Amoré, our one and only daughter:
I wish to thank you both for your support through more than
twenty-six years of ministry. You have served me in so many
ways, not always knowing where our destiny would take us.
Thanks for all your love and willingness to embrace with me
the promises of God for our future. Together we have served
many unknown camels, and our present status in ministry
proves that most of them were sent by God Himself. Your faith
in serving the Great Commission with me was our best decision ever. Thanks for serving His call upon our family.

To Sherie Campbell (who has maintained our web site, is responsible for the monthly design and processing of all GNN
partner newsletters and does the designs for our CDs as they
become available): Aside from Naomi and Amoré, you have
become the person who has most intensely served this ministry. We love you and will probably never be able to reward you
enough, but your ride to destiny is assured. We thank God
daily for you and the way in which you serve us.

To all missionaries worldwide: I want to thank God for the
thousands of men and women all over the world who are serving at the wells of responsibility, and are doing it for what they
believe is the highest calling in life. Missionaries are like
Rebekah at the wells of life, serving water to millions of thirsty
people. You have served well, and your ride to destiny will
come because of your faithful service to the nations.

ACKNOWLEDGMENTS

McDougal & Associates: Thank God for the giftings He has invested in His people. I wish to thank Harold McDougal personally for taking this book and making it say what it needed to say. Thanks, Harold, for becoming an extended hand to hear my heart and finish off this work—getting it ready for people out there everywhere. Your calm way of approaching the work is inspirational.

Abundant Life Assembly of God, Marion, Ohio: Where do I start in thanking Pastors Doug and Beverly Ford and their congregation? When I came to the U.S. in 1997 and began finding my way into the church world, Doug Ford discovered me and opened many doors for our ministry. Today, after nine years, he and the church have taken on the responsibility of this book and have sponsored most of the cost of it. Thank you, Pastors Doug and Beverly, for your endless love and compassion for our ministry and future. May thousands be blessed because of you and your people. May God bless Abundant Life Assembly of God in Marion, Ohio, for they made it happen.

Sherie Campbell: Sherie, who for years programmed our website and still does our newsletters, designed the cover for this book. Thanks, Sherie, for a job well done. You're a gift to us in so many ways.

CONTENTS

FOREWORD BY NEVIL NORDEN

In the Bible, God speaks to us in types and symbols. A symbol is a representation (one thing represents another), and a type is a prophetic representation (one thing is a preceding representation of another thing). In this book, André masterfully uses types, and I encourage you to walk with him as he walks with the biblical men and women of faith.

André operates in the office of a prophet, and this book is put together in a prophetic manner, to train and encourage every follower of Christ to fulfill his or her destiny by being faithful in the seemingly unimportant things of life. The seemingly unimportant things have always played a great role in my own life, so I love the way in which André prophetically uses them to take you along with him on a journey that will lead you to the prophetic fulfillment of your life's dreams and your God-ordained destiny.

Show me a man or woman who is faithful in the little, seemingly unimportant things of life, and I will show you a man or a woman of great faith, one who can be entrusted with much. This book is a prophetic challenge to be that man or woman.

Nevil Norden
Senior Pastor and founder of Living Word Ministries
South Africa

FOREWORD BY
DR. WALTER SNYMAN

This book is a blessing and, like a mirror, it reflects so much André's own trials and tests. The apostle Paul wrote to the Galatians (and to us), encouraging them (and us) not to grow weary in well doing, for, he said, in due season—meaning sooner or later—they (and we) would reap if they (and we) did not faint. Too often we do faint at the great challenge of the task before us, not knowing what a mighty reward awaits us, and we, therefore, come up short.

In this book, the author challenges us to review our attitude of readiness and willingness to serve wherever God sets us. We cannot expect to reap if we fail to sow or to endure until our time of reaping comes.

And, there is always an appointed time for the unveiling of God's plan and the whole purpose of the testing we have been enduring, and we must not give up before that moment arrives. I pray that the reading of this book may bring you light in every area of your life as you identify with its profound message.

Dr. Walter Snyman
Senior Pastor Lighthouse Ministries
Cape Town, South Africa

FOREWORD BY JOHANNES AMRITZER

This book, written by my good friend André van Zyl, contains a prophetic revelation presented to us in a simplicity that shows that it is genuinely inspired by the Spirit of Jesus of Nazareth. I was so blessed by the manuscript that I started to teach this pearl of insight and wisdom even before I finished reading the material. This is far more than ink on paper; it is the testimony of a man's life and the lessons he learned the hard and stinky way—feeding camels.

The work of the precious Holy Spirit in our lives is something we understand so much better after reading a teaching like this. Thank God for the camels André feeds and all the camels that will be fed as a result of the many readers who will then pursue their God-given destinies.

I love André, and I cannot wait for more of his books to be published with the same powerful, impacting and life-coaching spiritual teaching as this one. I encourage every reader: treasure this book, and consider it a diamond ring of knowledge on the finger of God in the end-time battle for the extension of Jesus' Kingdom on earth.

Johannes Amritzer
President, Evangelical Mission SOS International
Stockholm, Sweden

FOREWORD BY DAVID L. THOMAS

In André van Zyl's latest book, *Feed the Camels,* many lessons are presented, but one statement acts as a springboard of revelation:

> *The camels that will irritate you and complicate your life will also become your ride to destiny, and ignoring the camels in life is to ignore your very future.*

My dear friend has brought great spiritual truths to light from the seemingly mundane. Camels are rather homely creatures that often smell as bad as they look, and yet, as the quote indicates so powerfully, they can move us toward our destiny. May you be moved toward your destiny by this latest book from a man God is using mightily in the earth today.

David L. Thomas
Senior Leader
Victory Christian Center
NxL Network

INTRODUCTION

Dear Reader, I would like to invite you to join me on an exciting journey through ancient biblical times. If you choose to go along, together we will explore many wonderful revelations concerning the great patriarch Abraham, his son Isaac, his most trusted servant Eleazar and his daughter-in-law to be, Rebekah (the God-ordained bride of Isaac).

On this journey, we will also bump into some camels that belonged to Abraham, camels that constantly make their appearance in the Genesis account. Where do these camels fit in? They have a very interesting part to play in the current story, and they also play a major role in the future of Rebekah.

In order to understand the truths reflected in this book, you need to see all the above personalities (as well as the camels) as types. The most important types we will discover as we proceed are these: Abraham, a type of our heavenly Father; Isaac, a type of the Son of God—Jesus, the Bridegroom; Eleazar, a type of the Holy Spirit; and Rebekah, a type of the Church, the Bride of Christ, the servant. As for those camels, they were a type of the seemingly unimportant, or mundane, things in your everyday life. Don't despise them, for they come bearing hidden treasures.

With an emphasis on serving throughout the book, only unimportant and irritating camels, representing every challenge life may throw your way, could become a true test of servanthood. This is important, for the word *serve* has become one of the most unpopular words of our time, and the sudden appearance of ten arrogant and backbiting camels could put any true servant to the test.

Come now, and let us see what our heavenly Father has in store for you and me in these very exciting days of the twenty-first century and how He has called us to serve in the days ahead.

André van Zyl
Dacula, Georgia

CHAPTER 1

BLESSED IN ALL THINGS

The LORD had blessed Abraham in all things.

Genesis 24:1

The main character in our story is Rebekah, for she represents those of us who have made a decision to be part of Christ's Church, but we first need to place the focus of the book where it belongs. The foundation of all that we will discuss in the coming pages is found in the truth of this verse, and it begins with *"the Lord."* The key to greatness can be seen as the gift of God in us, but the real key is God Himself.

In this story, Abraham represents God. He was a type of our heavenly Father, and without Him there would be nothing worth writing about. It is *"in Him"* that *"we live and move and have our being"* (Acts 17:28). He is the very substance of our lives, and unless we have Him, the Source of all life, we simply have no real life at all. He is the Light, and unless we have Him, we have no real light at all. He is the genesis of all good things, and without Him, nothing good could or would exist.

Blessed "in All Things"

Abraham, as a type of God the Father, was *blessed in all things.*" This denotes that there was no emptiness, no limitations and no restrictions to be found in God. The fact that He is *blessed in all things*" means that nothing has been left out. He is complete, and we, therefore, can be complete in Him. Unless our blessings come from a source like this one, we will always have limited blessings.

> *Unless our blessings come from a source like this one, we will always have limited blessings!*

The blessings that would later come to the life of Rebekah had their genesis in the fact that Abraham was a blessed man himself. This is an important point. If we are to receive blessings from God's hand, we need to first know that He possesses what we need.

If there had been a limited blessing upon Abraham, then the blessings that flowed to others through him would also have been limited. The amount of water we can access is limited by how much is in the reservoir at any given time, and the quality of the water we access is determined by the quality of the water in the reservoir. A reservoir that contains contaminated water can only supply contaminated water.

BLESSED IN ALL THINGS

Thank God that He is our Source, for He is perfect and complete, and there is nothing lacking in Him. Therefore, if we receive what is in God, we will receive everything that we need. In Him, there is no lack or need, and He has made Himself available as our personal reservoir. The level of your blessing can never exceed the level of the source from which it comes. It is the resource of the blesser that determines how much you can receive. That's why you must make God your Source. Abraham's blessing from God included everything he needed, and because He was a type of our loving heavenly Father, our blessing can also overflow.

The Scriptures indicate that in God there is *"no variation or shadow"*:

Every good gift and every perfect gift is from above, and comes down from the Father of lights, with whom there is no variation or shadow of turning.

James 1:17

We understand what it means when it says that there is no *"variation"* in God, but what does it mean by the fact that there is no *"shadow"* in Him? Perfect light casts no shadows, and God is the perfect light.

As our Source, because God is, we are, and because He has, we also have. When He blessed Abraham, He gave him everything he needed, and He wants to do the very same for you and me today.

God's Intention for the Human Race

God's intention for the human race was that we should have everything we needed. Why would He have all things and then bless Abraham only with certain things? When man blesses, he does so with certain limitations, and rightly so, because he is limited. But God has no boundaries. He forgives our sins and, when He does, He removes them *"as far as the east is from the west"* (Psalm 103:12). Think about that. *"As far as the east is from the west"* ... how far is that? Our finite minds cannot answer such a question. It is beyond us, but not beyond God. Nothing is beyond Him. He is limitless.

When God told Abraham about the intensity, the width and the depth of the blessing that would come upon him, He used a calculator that no man before or since has ever used. In order to give Abraham an understandable sum total of that blessing, God used what I have come to call the stars-of-the-heaven calculator:

> *I will bless you, and multiplying I will multiply your descendants as the stars of the heaven and as the sand which is on the seashore; and your descendants shall possess the gate of their enemies.* Genesis 22:17

God was not satisfied with His stars-of-the-heaven calculator, so He next used a bigger one. I call this calculator the sand-on-the-seashore calculator. God has blessings planned for you and for me that go far beyond anything we can think of.

Stop for a moment and imagine the sum total of the stars of heaven plus the sand on the seashore. We all need to come to a higher level of understanding of the mightiness of the God we serve. He is boundless and limitless. If that were not overwhelming enough, there's more.

THE PRINCIPLES OF MULTIPLICATION

Still not satisfied, God combined His stars-of-the-heaven calculator and His sand-of-the-seashore calculator and then went even further. He now promised Abraham a multiplication principle (and this promise is for us too, who are the sons of Abraham by faith). God has promised that He will multiply our blessings, and multiplication is a very powerful principle. Ten plus ten equals twenty, but ten times ten equals one hundred. Addition is wonderful, but multiplication is much more wonderful.

God was not satisfied with the stars of the heaven, and He added to that the sand of the seashore. Then, He was not satisfied with merely adding blessings to our lives. Instead, He wants to multiply our blessings.

As Christians, we often speak about the double-portion blessing that the prophet Elisha sought, and we seek God for a similar blessing. But why is it that we rarely (or never) refer to the multiple blessings that came upon Abraham? We need to believe God for these blessings too.

A simple double portion was not enough for New Testament times. When Jesus stood before a crowd of four thousand men (plus their women and children), and He had only a small lunch of five loaves of bread and two fish to work with, adding to that or even doubling it would not have provided enough to feed so many people. If He had doubled what He had to work with, there would have been ten loaves of bread and four fish. And that wasn't even a drop in the bucket compared to what was needed.

No, in this case, Jesus had to use the multiplication method. Through the power of multiplication, He turned five loaves of bread and two small fish into more than enough food for some fifteen thousand people. Why do I say it was more then enough? Because there were twelve baskets left over, one for each of the doubting disciples. So why would you seek for a simple double blessing, when you could have a multiplied blessing?

The blessing of multiplication changed a small jar of oil owned by a Shunamite woman into a veritable refinery, and she was able to pay her debts and still have enough left over to live on for the rest of her life.

Multiplication was one of the abilities God gave to Adam and Eve way back in the very beginning of time. It was lost through sin, but it can be regained through faith in Christ today.

When Jesus revealed Himself in the New Testament, He remained true to character. He was still in the multiplying business.

The disciples tried to convince the Lord to send the hungry multitude away. After all, they were in a deserted, or lonely, place, and there were no stores to buy food.

This was a unanimous decision on the part of the disciples. They all agreed. This shows us clearly that just because a decision is unanimous on the part of man doesn't mean that God agrees with it.

The problem was clear: they had only five loaves of bread and two fish, and they had four thousand men to feed, plus their families. How could this be done? The wonderful thing is that even though we have limitations, God has none. Our limitations never hinder Him. He showed this by multiplying the disciples right out of their problem. Think about that. A double-portion blessing can still have limitations, but a multiplied blessing always provides leftovers.

God blessed Israel in the wilderness with manna from Heaven. He fed them every day, three-hundred and sixty-five (or six) days a year, and there was always more than enough food to go around. Some have estimated that the nation of Israel numbered some two million people at that time, and others have estimated that there were even more of them.

> *Just because a decision is unanimous on the part of man doesn't mean that God agrees with it!*

Whatever the case, they all ate and were filled, and there was food left over. The power of multiplication has no limits, and it lifts us into a realm of blessing that is difficult to comprehend.

ALL BLESSINGS FLOW FROM THE FATHER

The reason Abraham was blessed *"in all things"* was the fact that the God who blessed him was the Source from which all things come. This abundance was then seen in Abraham, a type of the Father. Had it not been for Abraham, Eleazar would have had no mission, Isaac would not have received a bride, and Rebekah would never have married and become fruitful.

Even the camels (that played such a significant role in this drama) would have had no significance at all were it not for the blessings of Abraham. What made the camels so important was the fact that they carried the gold and silver of Abraham. Had it not been for his gold and silver, the camels would have had nothing meaningful to carry. Abraham's blessings even made the camels look good.

Everything that is good comes from our Father, and we must come to understand that it is never about us. We are what we are and we have what we have only because of who and what our God is. His goodness is so incredible that even camels, creatures not made in the image of God, could become carriers of blessing and, thus, serve the purposes of the Almighty.

So, don't despise the camels in your life. The things that may seem to be camel-like (because they irritate you so much) could actually be the beginning of something great. Never be fooled by the wrapping in which your blessings come. (We'll have much more on this subject later in the book.)

God's promise of blessing to the people of Israel was powerful, and because it became part of His Word to His people of all ages, we can claim every word of it. Here's a sample of what God said:

> *Now it shall come to pass, if you diligently obey the voice of the Lord your God, to observe carefully all His commandments which I command you today, that the Lord your God will set you high above all the nations of the earth.* Deuteronomy 28:1

In the succeeding verses, Moses described how these blessings would flow down to us. God would bless our bodies, our children, our lands, our herds, our cattle and much more.

GOD'S SURPRISES

The blessing that came from Abraham to Rebekah was not a blessing that she had asked for, prayed for or even hinted at. She had no idea it was coming her way. It happened because there was a desire in the heart of Abraham to find a wife for his son Isaac.

Of course, the idea for this blessing originated with God. He desired to do good for Abraham long before Abraham knew that God had such a thing in mind.

For his part, Abraham made the first move in order to bless Rebekah. This is a type of our salvation that was a move on God's part to bless us—even before we considered serving Him. If He had not made that suggestion, there would be no way for us to receive salvation today. The One who has all things was the One who had to make a decision about what He wanted to do with His blessings.

Some people I know today may have a million dollars, but I could never force them to give it to me. With salvation, it was God who made that first move. He initiated the plan of salvation and then sent Jesus into the world to implement it. All good things are from His hand.

Now, with that proper foundation in place, let us depart on our journey, knowing that there are no limitations in God, and let us see what His approach will be toward us in order to bless us.

To all who dare to make this journey, let me issue this little warning. God often hides His blessings on the backs of camels. It was only toward the end of her journey that Rebekah would come to understand and appreciate more fully this great truth.

CHAPTER 2

TAKE A WIFE FOR MY SON ISAAC

So Abraham said to the oldest servant of his house, who ruled over all that he had, "Please, put your hand under my thigh, and I will make you swear by the Lord, the God of heaven and the God of the earth, that you will not take a wife for my son from the daughters of the Canaanites, among whom I dwell; but you shall go to my country and to my family, and take a wife for my son Isaac."   Genesis 24:2-4

Eleazar was not just the oldest of Abraham's servants; he was also the most trusted servant and the man Abraham chose to seek a bride for his son Isaac. It was a task that Abraham normally would have done himself, but he trusted Eleazar enough to assign him the responsibility instead.

The Scriptures also state that this servant *"ruled over all that he [Abraham] had,"* showing us clearly the extremely close relationship that existed between the two men. The relationship between Abraham and Eleazar speaks of the relationship between God the Father and the Holy Spirit. They work together to bring about a desired end.

Eleazar Must Have Known the Heart of Abraham

Eleazar must have known the heart of Abraham for Abraham to trust him fully with this delicate and important task. Choosing a life partner for his son was among the greatest responsibilities of Abraham's lifetime. The mutual understanding and cooperation between these two men, therefore, must have been phenomenal.

The mission of Eleazar came from the heart of Abraham, and when Eleazar left on the mission, no one could keep him from having success. He had to succeed, for he represented a powerful and wealthy man.

The Spirit of God is on a similar mission today. He is in the earth seeking a suitable bride for Jesus. This mission will be (and already is) successful. God, the Father, has full confidence in the Holy Spirit to seek and find just the right mate. And the Holy Spirit, just as Eleazar, knows the heart of the Father so well that when He (the Spirit of God) will present the Church to Him (God the Father), the Father will be impressed, and the Bride will be accepted.

If you wish to be part of the Bride, you must meet the requirements, and the Holy Spirit knows exactly what those requirements are. One of the chief duties of the Spirit in the earth today is to convince, or convict, us of our sins. He knows that in order to become part of the

Bride of Christ, we must be washed in the Blood of the Lamb.

With all this in mind, Eleazar left the house of his master with one intention—to fulfill the desire of Abraham and to bring back to Him exactly what He was asking for.

Abraham had made his servant swear an oath, stating that he would not choose a pagan bride for Isaac. She must come from the same family. This was an oath between two men, but if there ever was an oath that could not be broken, it is the oath between God the Father, Jesus the Son and the Holy Spirit.

Jesus said:

> *Eleazar had to succeed, for he represented a powerful and wealthy man!*

It is actually best for you that I go away, because if I don't the Counselor won't come. If I do go away, he will come because I will send him to you. And when he comes, he will convince the world of its sin, and of God's righteousness, and of the coming judgment.

When the spirit of truth comes, he will guide you into all truth. He will not be presenting his own ideas; he will be telling you what he has heard. He will tell you about the future. John 16:7-8 and 13, NLT

FEED THE CAMELS

The Holy Spirit has already found many members of the Bride of Christ, and He will continue to work on the completion of this enormous task until the day the Father decides the Bride is, at last, ready.

On the journey to find a bride for Isaac, Eleazar rode on the back of one of those camels we'll meet in the next chapter. The camels were carrying many gifts. This would eventually play a significant role in the entire affair.

When he arrived in the country he was sent to, Eleazar positioned himself at the well. He believed this was the place he could be most successful. Once there, he prayed to God and asked Him to make him successful. His strategy was this: He would look for a sign. The young woman who offered to give his camels water would be the chosen one. The idea was to find someone who had the heart of a servant. Such a woman would be a worthy bride for Isaac.

As we shall see, it was a test, and a very challenging one. Watering so many camels was an enormous task and one that only someone with a servant's heart could accomplish.

As we noted at the outset, the camels are a type of the unimportant things in life, and serving the camels faithfully illustrates and demonstrates the heart of a true servant. Let us now meet the camels and the woman who volunteered so willingly to serve them.

CHAPTER 3

TEN OF HIS MASTER'S CAMELS

Then the servant took ten of his master's camels and departed.   Genesis 24:10

We haven't gotten to anything substantial about Rebekah yet, but we will. The revelation of the camels and their purpose will serve to reveal Rebekah. First we have to introduce the camels.

Camels? Why would the Bible take time and space to mention these vile beasts? Anyone who knows much about camels knows that they are smelly and obstinate creatures, not at all pleasant to be around. Although camels do not live in every part of the world, most of us have seen a camel at some point—if only in a zoo. For the most part, what we know about camels is not good. They are not only smelly creatures; they are also loud and boisterous, often pitting their will against their owners or their drivers. Camels are very demanding, and, if they don't get their way, they often resort to biting the person nearest to them. In short, camels are not very nice to be around, and that's why more of us don't keep them for pets. They are not warm and cuddly creatures; they are obstinate and offensive.

> *God's blessings just may come to us on the backs of things we don't much care for and would rather avoid altogether!*

THE PURPOSE OF THE CAMELS

As unpleasant as they were, the camels had an important part to play. They were the means Abraham used to get his servant to where he was going, the means the servant used to bring with him the important gifts he carried for the prospective bride and the means used to bring back the bride to the wedding. Because, as we have noted, they are a type of the seemingly unimportant, or mundane, things of our daily lives, this is very important to us. The Holy Spirit (represented by Eleazar) comes to us accompanied by the irritations of life (represented by the camels) and is ready to bless us through them. God's blessings just may come to us on the backs of things we don't much care for and would rather avoid altogether.

In addition to the obvious uses for the camels Eleazar took with him, these animals served an even more vital purpose.

They became the test that would qualify Rebekah to be chosen as Isaac's bride. If she was willing to water them, she would be chosen, and if not, then she would not. Since we all want to be part of the glorious Bride of Christ and be joined to Him for eternity, this is something we all need to know about.

Here are some important things for us to consider about camels, as we examine them as types of the things that irritate us on a regular basis and also have the potential to carry to us God's finest blessings.

CAMELS CANNOT COMMUNICATE AS HUMANS DO

Eleazar's camels could not communicate in the normal way, but although they could not talk and respond as human beings, they still played a major role. They were divinely set in place for a specific purpose.

As we have noted, camels can become very demonstrative and demanding, and it is often the seemingly unimportant things in life that seem to demand our attention on a daily basis. For our part, we use every excuse available to avoid them.

If you could communicate with the things that irritate you, it might conceivably bring some relief. At the very least, you would have some chance of reasoning with whatever is nagging you. But these camels could not talk, so there was no reasoning with them.

Many times the things that most test your patience are those that cannot be removed by force or reason. They may be things you want and can't seem to get, or they may be things you never asked for, but they come to you anyway—without invitation. Reasoning with them will not make them disappear. They are there for a purpose—to test you and see what you're made of.

If we could reason with what irritates us, we might have a chance of winning the argument. But God will sometimes allow irritating things to come into our lives just to test us. How we treat each particular irritation will then determine whether or not we can move on in life.

Rebekah was not called to reason with the camels, just to give them a drink. Don't try to communicate when what you need to do is serve. If she had insisted on talking with the camels, she would not have been able to do what was expected of her. Her duty was to serve them water, nothing more.

Because the camels could not communicate, in the end, Rebekah would not receive so much as a thank-you for her services, so willingly rendered. This, in itself, was a test. In situations like this, our immediate tendency is to want to give someone a piece of our mind. But be careful. These are true tests of your character.

CAMELS REQUIRE LARGE AMOUNTS OF WATER

Hand in hand with the frustrations we face in life goes a certain demanding aspect that only frustrates us further. Nothing is more frustrating than someone or something that is always demanding something of us— our time, our attention or our energy.

Because camels have the ability to go for long periods

of time without water, when they do drink, they drink an amazing amount of water. They actually have two stomachs, and they are both large. How many trips would that have been for Rebekah with her pitcher? She had come to the well to draw water for herself, so she wasn't prepared for the massive task of supplying all those thirsty camels. They were not able to ask for water in the human way, but everyone knew how much of it they needed. When reaching any camp, that was always one of the first considerations. "We must water the camels."

A farmer who has oxen or cows or any other type of livestock always has to be thinking of their welfare. It's amazing how things that are considered to be unimportant in life can begin to consume all of our available time and energy.

In many cases, you didn't ask for this to happen. It just did. But how you react to it reveals your true make up. It is what we do under pressure (when no one is watching) that reveals who we really are.

Water is what keeps both man and beast alive, and we all need it. Still, Rebekah didn't ask for these camels to come along just then, and she probably had no intention of performing such a service that day when she set out for the well. The camels just showed up, and for some reason, with having to be asked, Rebekah took them on as her personal responsibility. She felt compelled to serve them the needed water.

When you have what others need, but are under no obligation to give it to them, will you do it? Too often, we demand some sort of payment in return before we're willing to act. Rebekah didn't wait to be asked, and she asked nothing in return. There was a need, and she set about to meet that need. She offered her services, offered to give the camels what they needed, offered to serve them willingly. Again, it's the seemingly unimportant things in your life, things that just show up on their own, suddenly becoming your responsibility, that ultimately become the carrier of your greatest surprises.

It is basically impossible to go through life without meeting demanding issues. These demanding issues have nothing to do with what has gone wrong, but they have everything to do with how you will respond to them. Demanding camels, or demanding situations, just might become rewarding camels, or rewarding situations, for you. Your greatest obstacle in life can become your bridge to the land of promise.

CAMELS BITE

Camels are known to bite, and your ultimate crisis might come when the things in life you never asked for but have decided to feed anyway, turn, and without warning, suddenly attack you. That will give you a double reason to back out of your commitment.

I didn't ask for this.
This is not what I ordered.
Who told you to come here?
Why is this happening to me?

Something like this is what we say when things start going wrong. How can you remain faithful in service when those you are serving suddenly start attacking you? Far too often, the thing you bless with water today will turn and bite you tomorrow, and it's just another test of your character.

How many times have the people in whom you have invested your life let you down? It happens, and it happens often. If your enemy lets you down, you can understand that. If your enemy bites at you or tries to harm you, that can be expected. But when camels you never asked for become your responsibility, and you begin to give them water, and then tomorrow they bite at you, that's much more difficult to understand.

It is basically impossible to go through life without meeting demanding issues!

Expect the worst from the unexpected, unknown, smelly and biting irritations that come to your life. You can't afford to ignore them, simply because you don't know to whom they belong or what they carry on their backs. Remember that your greatest surprises are hidden on the back of your greatest frustrations. It is the biting camels of today that will blow kisses of blessings at you in your tomorrows. With this in mind, we all need to have the right approach: serve, no matter what it costs because the reward is always much greater than the sacrifice. The size of your service and sacrifice will always pale in comparison with the size of your blessing, when God eventually reveals it.

THESE CAMELS HAD A SIGNIFICANT OWNER

Could it be that such unimportant camels had an important owner? Who sent these camels? And to whom did they belong? We know that Eleazar had brought the camels (or they had brought him), but he was not their owner. They belonged to Abraham.

In the meantime, they were irritating. Many times, the way the Holy Spirit is working in your life will not seem to be understandable. The very thing that you think of as a curse is actually, in its final form, a blessing. Joseph's pit turned into a palace, and your irritations can become your means of exaltation as well.

These camels, that could easily have been ignored by Rebekah as unworthy of her attention, were the property of Abraham. Abraham, as we have seen, was *"blessed in all things,"* and part of that blessing was his camels. He was the richest man in his part of the world at the time and may well have been the richest man on the face of the earth.

It is so easy for us to avoid things that look bad to us at first sight, not realizing that they may actually carry a rich blessing for us. These normal-looking camels came from one of the richest men on earth. How amazing is that? What could have been seen as an irritation was actually a benefit in disguise. And there are many things in each of our lives that we see as an irritation, when they are actually sent by God to bring us a surprising blessing.

The camels may not have seemed worthy of Rebekah's time and attention, but she had no way of knowing the significant role they would play in her life. We don't know everything either, so we should be careful how we treat the people around us and how we view them. It might be your greatest enemy who carries your greatest blessing. Trust God. A painting is never finished until the artist signs it, and God's not finished with your life yet, so don't be too quick to judge the final outcome.

Let's understand this well. The things that are a frustration to one are a blessing to another. The same camels that were a frustration to Rebekah were a blessing to Abraham. That, in itself, is a powerful truth. Jesus, who irritates the devil to no end, was and still is a blessing to us. It's all in the way you look at it.

The value of the camels became evident once it was known to whom they belonged. Camels that belong to a poor owner can only carry poverty on their backs, but camels belonging to millionaires just might be carrying gold and silver. It is not the significance of the camels that is important, but the significance of their owner. By serving the camels, Rebekah was actually serving Abraham, the richest man around. And, since she was to become the bride of Abraham's heir, she would benefit from her future father-in-law's fortune.

The blessing of Abraham was to become the blessing of his descendants, and that made the camels worthy of attention. Would we serve differently if we had complete knowledge of where our camels came from? How many things would we have done differently if we'd only had insight into the importance of our every action, however insignificant they may have seemed at the time?

> *Would we serve differently if we had complete knowledge of where our camels came from?*

Your life may appear to be insignificant, and often you may feel no more important than a camel. But the One who bought us with His own blood on the cross of Calvary made us worthy. If it were not for Him, we would all have been like camels, strolling through life biting, smelling bad and demanding constant attention. Now we are His, and we still may not look very good, but what we have on the inside of us, Christ's investment into our lives, will soon be revealed to the world. When that happens, the whole world will have to admit that the Church carries in her bosom the gold and silver and the other goods they so desperately need.

Open your mouth, and unload your gift. Let the world

see that you and I were sent on a divine mission to surprise them with the greatest message ever spoken, the Gospel of Jesus Christ. We did not call ourselves, and we cannot appoint ourselves. What we have accomplished and what we will accomplish in the future is all because of our Master. He is the significant One. He is our Source, the Man behind the scenes.

Who is behind the scene changes everything? Many times we see things representing great riches displayed before us: skyscrapers, jet airplanes, gold mines or oil wells, etc. The amazing thing to think about is that all of those belong to someone. Most of us will probably never meet those owners, but when it comes to God, the Creator of everything, we have an invitation to meet Him and even live with Him. He is the Man behind the scene, and He made all the things others think they own. Somehow, if we serve well, at the right time, we will be recognized, just like Rebekah, and we, too, will be amply rewarded.

THESE CAMELS CARRIED SPECIAL GIFTS

As we have noted, on the backs of these camels, items of gold and silver and other precious gifts were carried. These were special gifts, and they were being carried on the backs of otherwise unimportant camels. The gifts had been handpicked for a very special lady, and only one woman would qualify to receive them.

Other men accompanied Eleazar and, like him, they rode on the camels. The men were visible, but the special gifts that also rode the camels were not. These gifts were kept hidden, to be opened and disbursed at just the right time to just the right person. During the trip, the gifts remained safe, because they were hidden on the backs of the seemingly insignificant animals.

Many times the greatest gifts are to be found in the desert. A great part of the world's reserves of gold and diamonds are to be found in Africa, the continent many still call the Dark Continent. It seems that God decided to hide a great part of the wealth of the earth in a place where no one would ever expect to look for it.

CAMELS SERVE US BEST WHEN WE ARE WEAK

Camels are especially good at carrying heavy loads through the desert. Many times, there would be no other way to get those goods through. And your greatest blessing just might come on the back of a camel. Sometimes the only way for God to deliver your gift is through frustrations.

Maybe there are deserts that seem to separate you from your blessing or your connection to destiny. But God owns a camel that can connect you to the beauty of your destiny, and no desert will keep you from that—if you're willing to serve the unimportant things of life.

Rebekah surely never imagined that while watering the camels she was making a way for her ride into destiny. Camels are often called the Cadillacs of the desert, and nothing could serve man better in those harsh circumstances. For the most part, no man would challenge a desert without some camels, for they seem to have been expressly designed for this purpose. The feet of a camel were designed by God to carry heavy loads over scorching sand, and Rebekah had some harsh territory to cross to get to her beloved. The camels she cared for were to become her destiny ride to meet her bridegroom.

Our difficulties could easily become our ride to something better. Not everything that appears to be bad will end badly. Frustration can easily become the bridge to happiness. The camels knew the way back to Abraham. They traveled a way that was unknown to Rebekah, but because they had knowledge of the desert, she had nothing to fear. They could take her where she could not otherwise go.

If treated well, these animals would serve Rebekah by giving her a ride. The frustration that you serve today will serve you in your desert tomorrow. If you will serve water to the camels today, they will serve comfort to you in an upcoming season of challenge. They will keep your feet from burning in the hot sand.

Many people can only serve well when everything is to their advantage. Rebekah knew how to sacrifice.

Your camels will serve you well in a season in which you would normally have suffered. Camels and men, it seems, were made for each other. Men need camels, just as camels need men.

CAMELS HAVE A BEAUTY ALL THEIR OWN

Beautiful? What could be beautiful about a camel?

Where is the beauty to be found in such an animal? Usually beauty, whether in man or beast, is only revealed once the particular gift is revealed. In themselves, camels have no beauty, but their beauty is revealed once they operate in the realm for which they were designed.

The beauty of an athlete is seen in running a hundred-meter race in the Olympics. The beauty of a jet fighter is seen when it is able to defend against an encroaching enemy. The beauty of a servant is seen only when the act of serving is in operation. The beauty of a prophet is seen only when he or she is prophesying. In the same way, the beauty of a camel is seen only when he rescues a man by carrying him through the desert. In that moment, a man has nothing but compliments for his beloved beast. "Only a camel can do well in a desert," he says. "Nothing can beat it." Suddenly, he loves those smelly beasts.

Certain creatures were created for certain conditions. In these conditions, they fare better than any other creature. Rebekah was made to serve water to camels, and camels were created to save her in the desert. They needed each other.

Beauty can sometimes be found in strange places, and sometimes we search in vain for beauty in places where it will never be found. Your beauty is to serve well where no one else expects you to serve. By serving well in difficult places, your gift looks better. In serving, you take a position that not everyone can (or is willing to) take. You will perform acts that not everyone can (or will) perform.

The camel is even sometimes called the rose of the desert. Why? Because it lends beauty to a dry land when nothing else can. God made the earth, and when He did, He created a beauty that is not always understood by man.

The camel's eye was especially created for the sand storms that sometimes occur in the desert. When a storm arises, these amazing animals can continue to function normally. When desert winds begin to blow, a camel can see when no one else can. The camel can continue to move forward and function normally even when man's ability has come to its limits. A camel will flourish where other creatures, including man, would die. That's a beautiful thing.

> *When desert winds begin to blow, a camel can see when no one else can!*

The body of the camel was created to thrive in a difficult environment and to endure without water for long periods of time. God made this animal unique in order to serve in the desert.

If God used such precision when creating an animal to serve in the desert, how much more has He fitted you for a higher purpose! We can serve with excellence if we make sure to fit into the world that He created us for. Never insist on serving where you want to serve. Serve where God has placed you. To insist on serving where we want to serve is rebellion. To serve where God has positioned you is obedience.

Our lives were not designed to impress those around us. There is Someone behind the scenes who has His eye on us. He is our Owner, and that makes all the difference. As we have noted, there was nothing significant about these camels in themselves. What made them so important was the fact that they belonged to Abraham. The moment the name Abraham was connected to the camels, even smelly camels took on a whole new significance. They became beautiful.

CAMELS HAVE AN ETERNAL IMPORTANCE

How important can unimportant things become? If these so-called "unimportant" things were actually sent by God Himself, then it is impossible to overemphasize their importance. These humble camels played a very important role as they carried the hidden gifts from Abraham, so they had an eternal importance. Their significance was tied up in their owner. It had everything to do with their belonging to him.

When you get to know our heavenly Father, you will quickly learn that there is never such a thing as an unimportant day or an unimportant event in your life. Jesus taught us:

And whoever gives one of these little ones only a cup of cold water in the name of a disciple, assuredly, I say to you, he shall by no means lose his reward.

Matthew 10:42

After all, when we offer the person that cup of cold water, we are actually offering it to the Lord. Therefore, many of the details of our daily lives are far more important than we could ever imagine. Tending to camels? Giving them water? Becoming a servant to others when no one seems to be thankful? Those don't seem like very spiritual acts, but in doing them, we are making God's Kingdom to become a reality.

Everybody wants to be important and to be recognized, but the two are not necessarily connected. As we are learning, recognizing the unimportant could easily become the most important thing in our lives. God can easily hide Himself behind unimportant things.

But serve camels? Yes, a servant is never motivated by whom he serves. It is the act of service that is important. The act of serving is more important than the person being served. Some people can only serve when the person they are serving is a person of stature. But that is not the true mark of servanthood. The reason Rebekah passed the test was that she was willing to serve and serve well in a situation where most others would have failed. She passed the test because she was not led by what or whom she served. Rather, a spirit of service drove her to serve — no matter who was on the receiving end of her service.

Camels Function Best in Dry Places

Because of their special abilities, camels are often associated with deserts or other dry places. When you think of a camel, you think of the hot sun burning down without grace upon the desert sand. There is a truth for us to learn here.

> *The camels that show up in your life will always come during dry spells!*

The camels that show up in your life will always come during dry spells, just when you're sure you could have done better with something else. No one wants a camel, because they come with deserts. But think about it this way: when deserts come, thank God for the camels in your life.

In times of difficulties, it's the camels that will carry you through. It is the camel that can make a challenging ride in the desert a joyful one. You may not need a camel every day, but you cannot take on a desert without one. Remember, camels carry you through your desert to your destiny. In other words:

CAMELS + DESERTS = DESTINY

Don't miss your destiny because you refuse your camel.

Your Camel May Carry You To Your Destiny

It was the unimportant camels, that Rebekah could easily have ignored, that would ultimately carry her over the hot desert sands to her destiny. A camel would take her where she could not have otherwise gone.

Be careful how you treat things or people you think will amount to nothing. That person could easily surprise you and become the camel legs that will help you on your way to your future. Where your own abilities can't take you, unimportant things will.

So, are camels as unimportant as we might think? Not really. Rather than our scorn, camels are deserving of our respect. They are God's vehicles for good. Treat them well, and they'll give you a ride to your tomorrow.

CHAPTER 4

HIS MASTER'S GOODS

All his masters goods were in his hand.

Genesis 24:10

When Eleazar left the house of Abraham, he did not leave empty-handed. Abraham supplied him with everything he would need on his journey. Aside from the necessary provisions, he was to carry with him some very special blessings, blessings that were to be given only to the one who would be chosen to become the bride of Isaac.

As we have noted, it was the mission of Eleazar to find a bride for Isaac and to take her back with him to his land. But incredible blessings would be given to her even before she met Isaac and was joined to him in matrimony. These special blessings were carried to her land on the backs of the camels.

The eternal life that God offers to each of us is an incredible, even indescribable, blessing. God's intentions are for you and me to enjoy this blessing here on the earth long before we meet Him physically and are joined to Him for eternity. Too many among us have their sights set so firmly on Heaven that they fail to realize that the camels of everyday life are loaded with blessings God wants us to enjoy in the here and now.

Hidden Treasures

The hiding place for these special goods was significant (and this could become an important key for your life as well). The gifts sent by Abraham were concealed on the backs of the ten camels that had accompanied Eleazar. Sometimes the greatest blessings come to us in very strange ways.

As Eleazar traveled, he bore hidden treasure. His ten camels looked like ordinary beasts of burden. There was nothing about them that drew special attention. But inside their saddles were hidden these special gifts. If others had known what was there, they, too, would have offered to water the camels. It is the unimportant things in life that sometimes carry the most incredible surprises. They just come to us in strange packages or strange wrappings.

For the mission to find a bride, Abraham's camels were loaded with blessings, and in my own life I have also discovered that God hides His goods in strange places. Years ago, I had some definite conceptions about how God would fulfill His promises in my life. I was greatly surprise when many of those promises were fulfilled in the most remarkable and unexpected ways, and the blessings came from the most unexpected sources. The camels you are currently facing may have your surprise blessings on their backs.

Although physical camels are not found in every part of the world, we all have to deal with the particular camels we need to tend to in daily life. They will always appear unimportant and can be, therefore, very easy to ignore. But, as we now know, these particular camels belonged to Abraham, and they carried his goods. Others may not have appreciated their worth because: (1) The camels were not theirs, and (2) They didn't know what the camels were carrying. Those who knew had a very deep appreciation for the purpose of the camels.

> *If others had known what was hidden there, they, too, would have offered to water the camels!*

God's Gifts To Us

When God sends His Holy Spirit to us, He never comes empty handed. He bears many special gifts. But those gifts may be hidden among the mundane things of life.

Every time we open the Bible and begin to read about the goodness of God, it is overwhelming. An entire library could not contain the books needed to describe His benefits. More importantly, He loves each of us and wants to share with us His bounty.

Eleazar had come to seek a bride for his master, and he came with personal gifts for her, gifts that he began opening and imparting almost immediately. And the Holy Spirit of God is more loaded with goodness than we could ever imagine. His hands are overflowing with blessings that He desires to give His Church now in advance of our heavenly union with Christ.

Salvation through the blood of Jesus, made possible through the working of God's Spirit, is just the beginning of what God wants to do for us. After that, comes healing, deliverance, miracles, signs and wonders and many other blessings.

The treasures carried by the camels remained hidden until the bride could be identified. Only then would the gifts be revealed. In the same way, the Spirit of God has with Him gifts from the throne room of the Father, and His desire is for us to enjoy these gifts while we're still here on this earth. Do what you have to do to see them revealed.

Eleazar at the well is an important prophetic picture of how God is about to identify His Bride and how He will reveal His gifts to His Bride once she is identified. Get ready to tend to your camels, for they carry special treasures, divine surprises that are revealed only to those who are in the process, or act, of serving.

Gift Wrapping Is an Important Part of Our Giving

Gift giving is an important part of our social tradition. It's the way we show our love and appreciation for others. Because of that, we make an effort to wrap our gifts in very special papers and tie them with beautiful bows. I love to receive gifts, and when I see their special wrappings, I can hardly wait to open them and see what's inside. I'm sure you feel the same way. But sometimes we're disappointed.

I sometimes receive gifts from the people who are blessed in our meetings. Several times, when leaving a meeting, I couldn't wait to get back to the hotel room to open a gift I had been given, only to find nothing more than a few cookies inside. Oh, they were wonderful cookies, and I enjoyed them, but I couldn't help wondering if the wrapping paper hadn't cost more than the cookies themselves.

Don't get me wrong. We all know that it's not about the cost of the gift, but the idea behind it. But even with that in mind, we're always more interested in what's inside, and the packaging can be very misleading. In the case of the cookies, the wrapping drove my expectancy level so high that I somehow expected more than cookies and was then disappointed. When presented in a bright, shiny, and even glittering wrapping, gifts are very intriguing.

My wife has made it a habit to collect the wrappings from the gifts people give her. Why would she do that?

Because they're too beautiful to throw away. Sometimes the gift bag is with us long after the gift itself has been discarded or used up.

Not all gifts are worth the cost and effort. Still, we love our fancy gift wrappings. To my way of thinking, God does things in just the opposite way. He specializes in using what we might consider very poor wrappings, and He does this to disguise His blessing, so that He can maintain the element of surprise. His greatest blessings often come in the ways we least expect them.

> *When Jesus died, there was nothing impressive about it!*

THE UNIMPRESSIVE WRAPPING OF JESUS ON THE CROSS

Consider, for instance, the crucifixion of Jesus. There could not have been a more unattractive drama to unfold before your eyes. When Jesus died, there was nothing impressive about it. He died alone, His blood slowly draining from Him and water slowly seeping from His side. The only crown He wore that day was a crown of thorns. He did not make a favorable impression upon the world, and He did not look much like a Savior or a Healer.

The accusation made against Him that day was that He could not even deliver Himself from the cross, and that left the observers of the event no reason to believe that He could save the human race from Hell. How could this Man save the human race, when He couldn't even save Himself from the cross?

By the time He drew His last breath, our Lord had lost most of His friends, and even Peter, one of His closest disciples, had denied that he knew Him. This was not unusual. When the wrapping over your life becomes unattractive, you may be surprised how many of your friends will leave you and how quickly it will happen. Key to our understanding of God's blessings is the fact that the greatest of them sometimes come in the most unattractive wrappings we could ever imagine.

No worldly champion would choose to make his way onto the world stage in the unimpressive fashion Jesus did. The moment a man or woman achieves worldly fame, they are treated like royalty. They suddenly have special guards around them, and they have to be specially dressed for every occasion. They make their appearance in style and expect the world to handle them with kid gloves because they've "arrived."

The difference is that the wrapping of fame and fleshly honor is vain. Hollywood may be glamorous, but it's also empty and false. There is no substance in that kind of life once the wrapping has been removed. Never be misled by the outward appearance of someone. Never be drawn or impressed by the wrappings.

Jesus, the Son of the Living God, did not come to this earth in a fancy wrapping. He did not appear as a super-star, even though He was the Morning Star. He did not arrive in a Town Car with the glittering lights of fame and with television cameras surrounding Him. Still, although He didn't have that kind of wrapping over Him, what He brought us was of such importance that once the real gifts of salvation, healing and deliverance were received by the human race, the wrappings they came in suddenly didn't seem so unimpressive.

It was upon a rugged and despised cross that generation upon generation was saved. It was on that cross that generations were set free from their sins. It was on that cross that Hell was plundered and stripped of generations of souls. The cross of Jesus was the reason that many today are raised from the dead. The sting of death lost its power over the human race through the greatest of gifts, everlasting life purchased by Jesus on Calvary's ugly cross.

As the devil and his demons celebrated their apparent victory in the underworld, Jesus showed up, just before His resurrection on the third day, and He took back the keys of death and Hell. There is nothing on earth that could have added to the value of what was given to us on that cross, and yet it was not appealing at all to those who saw it.

Why use an impressive wrapping on a gift if the contents of the package are worth little or nothing? That's deceptive and leads to disappointment. When a gift is of sufficient value, it needs no special wrapping to enhance its beauty.

The cross of Calvary was unimpressive, but it carried

the most valued gift ever given to mankind. In fact, the riches of this world multiplied with the stars of heaven and the grains of sand on the earth cannot even be compared with what happened on that cross. Let it be known that God conceals His gifts in unimpressive wrappings.

Imagine what it would have been like if Jesus had been just another person who was only pretending to be the deliverer, coming in fleshly glory and manly honor, and then, once He had died it was discovered that He had just been another fake. How terrible that would have been! Give me the unimpressive, rejected, humiliated, lonely, blood, sweat and tears wrapping of that cross. I find in that wrapping my eternal destiny and my everlasting peace.

THE UNIMPRESSIVE WRAPPINGS OF JOSEPH

Joseph of Old Testament fame received a dream from God that he would become the Prime Minister of Egypt, but getting there proved more difficult and time consuming than he ever imagined. One of the captivating things about his story was the coat of many colors his father gave him when he was still very young. That coat became synonymous with Joseph. The problem was that God could not allow Joseph to depend on his coat, and He had to allow many hardships to come to his life to work some substance into the lad before he was ready to rule.

In his youth, Joseph was full of pride, and perhaps the coat of many colors only added to this prideful attitude.

Although he was covered in a very attractive coat, his character was not ready for a promotion. In the end, just before his promotion, he wasn't allowed to have any coat of any value. Instead, he became a man with a jail record—broken and rejected. In that moment, Joseph's outer covering had been completely destroyed, but the inner coat was now complete. It was only then that he found himself at the beginning of the fulfillment of his dream.

The coat had been impressive, but the thing that would carry Joseph through his trials and tests would be the substance worked into him through his various ordeals. He first fell into the hands of his angry and jealous brothers and landed in a pit. In the pit of circumstances, you need more than a coat to carry you through, and it was there in the pit that Joseph had to learn how to rely on the inner strength that God alone could give him. Outer beauty will always wear away, but substance has a beauty of its own that can never be destroyed. If you have substance, it will carry you into places where a fancy coat could never take you.

Joseph was stripped of his coat, and his brothers dipped it in blood and took it to their father, telling him that the lad had been killed by a lion. Let men destroy your outer coat of impressiveness, but allow God to wrap you in something more substantial. It may not impress this fashion conscious world in which we live, but it will impress the spirit world.

Jesus, although He did not impress the people around the cross, made an impression on Hell when He conquered death and took back the keys of death and Hell from the enemy. His own people ripped Him apart, and that's also what happened with Joseph. Then, Joseph, too, had to go into foreign territory to capture what the enemy had in his hand. When Jesus went into foreign territory, He became King and Prince on the earth and did it right in the face of the enemy. And just like Jesus, Joseph came to his glory under very unusual circumstances.

THE UNIMPRESSIVE BIRTH OF JESUS

If the place where Jesus was born was to be an indicator of who He was, the world could have easily been misled. A humble stable? That was not impressive at all.

God is so different from us. Men cannot always fill their fancy gift wrapping with an expensive gift, so they need to add some glitter and shine to the wrapping in

If the place where Jesus was born was to be an indicator of who He was, the world could have easily been misled!

order to impress the recipient and the onlookers. But God doesn't need a special wrapping, simply because what He puts on the inside needs no help from the outside to make an impression. No wonder God's greatest gifts always come from places where we would never have expected!

Jesus, the Son of God, was born in a place where not even the poorest of the poor would like their children to be born. But don't be put off by the stable. Don't be disappointed by the hay. Don't be sad that there was no crowd to welcome our Lord to this earth. You and I may need a crowd to look good, but Jesus, all by Himself, was a majority.

There was no special doctor waiting for Jesus' arrival, and He didn't have any medical insurance. His parents were just ordinary people, but what Mary carried in her bosom was of such significance that what the circumstances were played no role in the matter whatsoever.

When hearing about the birth of Jesus, King Herod and the people of Jerusalem were *"troubled"* (Matthew 2:3). The significance of the coming of this baby was so great that the announcement of His coming shocked the city—even before He was delivered. And God is about to show up in other places with such blessings that the satanic world will be stirred by their arrival—even before it takes place.

How and why would a small baby in a manger stir people in high places? Why would a whole city be troubled by His birth? It is difficult to imagine, but God will again stir the world in these last days by revealing His greatest surprises and demonstrating His power and authority, as He reveals Himself to this world.

Hollywood and the platforms of this world present their superstars, but their appearance never changes the world. What they have is nothing new; it's been seen before. Jesus is different. The Son of the Living God, who carries within Himself the seed of everlasting life and your healing and deliverance, will reveal Himself in these last days as a mighty force to be reckoned with.

A Hollywood superstar can never take you higher than the platform on which he or she operates. Jesus not only comes to identify Himself to us where we are; He also lifts us into a level of the heavenly where no man could ever take us. Perhaps His wrappings are unimpressive, but what He delivers to us is.

Many fine Christian people in this day are putting a remarkable amount of emphasis on professionalism, or the wrappings of our faith. There's nothing wrong with being professional, and I believe in being as professional as possible. But the danger is that we might become so professional that in the process of becoming and being professional we can lose the power of God. The moment professionalism takes precedence over the power of God we will have nothing left. To have the letter without the spirit will always bring death:

The letter kills, but the Spirit gives life.
2 Corinthians 3:6

How sad it is when we suddenly discover that in becoming organized we have also become empty. Again, please don't misunderstand what I'm saying. To become more organized and do things in excellence is an absolute necessity, but, at the same time, we must protect the substance of what comes to us from the Spirit. In the end, that's all that counts.

The real man is not the one all dressed up in the fancy suit. That's just the flesh that carries the real man around. The real you is who you are in the spirit. I've met corrupt people who were dressed up in very expensive clothing. If I had been led by what they wore, I could have made a big mistake. Let us be led by the Spirit, and let us discern what is real and what is fake.

> *The real man is not the one all dressed up in the fancy suit!*

Jesus chose not to be born in a palace, but in a humble manger. Yet He was God in the flesh.

THE UNIMPRESSIVE BIRTH OF THE FIRST CHURCH

The birth of the Church was just as unimpressive to the natural eye as the camels of Eleazar ever were. Somewhere in an upper room, not even belonging to them, a group of humble men and women, many of them fisher-men, got together to start the first church. How unimpressive could that be? There was no televised an-nouncement of the event, and no specific time was posted. And, since no one knew what the time of this birth would be, they couldn't prepare for it. All they could do was wait and see what happened.

The order of the procedures that day was not shared with anyone beforehand. The program was not printed, because no program was available. No one knew ahead of time what to expect—not even those who were present and would experience it. Why would the mighty God of Heaven and earth do things in such a disorderly way? We need to understand things so that we can report on them accurately, don't we? But God knows what we need bet-ter than we do.

In this case, what the Church needed would come in a way that many would have preferred to be different. Pen-tecost is still not understood by many people. Because no important people were involved and no announcement was made, the whole event could very easily have been ignored, just the way camels were commonly ignored. The problem is that you and I need what the Day of Pentecost provided, so we cannot afford to ignore it.

When the power came to the Church that day, it came *"suddenly"* (Acts 2:2). That means there was no warning, and no preparations could be taken. If it had not hap-pened in this way, *"suddenly,"* it would have given men and women time to think it through, and by the time they had discerned what it was, they would have rejected it. This is one of the greatest reasons God loves to deliver His gifts to us suddenly and unexpectedly. Then, He stands back to see what our reaction will be.

The things we most desperately need in our lives are often the things that come in such a way that we feel we have reason to reject them. God started His Church in an unprecedented and unorthodox way. We might choose to ignore it, but that could cost us our very lives. Many of the seemingly simple things in life have eternal destiny built into them.

The Church started with *"a rushing mighty wind"* (Acts 2:2). Next, there were *"tongues of fire"* that could be seen (Verse 3). Then the humble followers of Jesus spoke in languages they had never learned (Verse 4). From this came a new boldness, and Peter began preaching to those who gathered to see what was occurring. Three thousand of those listeners came to the Lord that day (Verse 41).

From the sudden visitation to the just-as-sudden newfound boldness of Peter, we have a chaotic picture before us. If we, the members of the Church today, had to vote on whether God should start His Church in this way, we would still be without a Church. The gifts and manifestations that come with Pentecost are not always acceptable to some people, and there's not a thing we can do about it. God has chosen to wrap His Church in unusual wrapping paper. The surprise lies waiting on the inside.

The Wrappings of the Seven Sneezes

There is an Old Testament story that presents us with some interesting wrapping. A certain Shunamite woman befriended the prophet Elijah and blessed him with room and board whenever he passed through her area. Elijah prayed for her to conceive a son, and she did.

When this miracle son suddenly died, the woman ran to Elijah to beg for his help. He willingly went to the room where the child was and prayed for him. But before the needed resurrection was realized, the Word of God states that the boy sneezed seven times (2 Kings 4:35). Now what was that all about?

Nobody loves sneezes, and although we all want resurrection power to come to the Church, we want it to come in such a way that it will not offend anyone. If anything is offensive, it's sneezes. Still, show me the mother who would prefer her child to be dead than to have a bedroom disturbed by sneezes.

When God moves, His power will be demonstrated, and the Church must come to grips with the fact that the wrappings He uses are not always impressive. In the end, the wrappings are not what's important. What's on the inside of the package is so desperately needed that we must look beyond the unimpressive wrapping. Give me the sneeze, as long as I can get my son back. Give me the unimpressive, as long as I can recover my daughter. Resurrection power is so needed in the Church that we can no longer afford to be put off by how God will send it.

We live in a very professional, very high-tech age, and

the Church of today is miles away from the Church of yesterday. There is nothing wrong with living in this particular day, and there is nothing wrong with all the comforts this day affords us. Still, we must keep in mind one important thing: the God of Abraham, Isaac and Jacob is the same God today as He was in years gone by. He will sometimes deliver our blessing in a wrapping we are not expecting. We must be renewed in ours minds to the point that we understand what we hear from God, even when we do not understand the wrapping it might come in.

Do you want to receive the *"master's goods"*? Then expect them to come to you on the backs of camels. That's just how God has chosen to do it.

CHAPTER 5

HE MADE HIS CAMELS KNEEL DOWN

*And he made his camels kneel down outside the city
by a well of water.*   Genesis 24:11

We now know a lot more about the camels that accompanied Eleazar, and, by now, we surely realize that they are a type of the seemingly unimportant, or mundane, things in our daily lives. Eleazar played a major role in this story, but the real test of faith for Rebekah had to do with the camels. If she had not been willing to give them water, she would have failed the test. That test was about to begin.

Serving those camels had nothing to do with Rebekah's ability or talents. Most anyone can draw and carry water. You don't need a university degree to do that. Still, as incredible as it seems, this simple test was one that most of us would have failed.

God knows how to present us with just the right tests, and often when the test is over, we laugh about how easy it has been, but nothing about it seems easy at the moment. Rebekah needed no special qualifications to meet her test. Water the camels. That was all that was required of her. And yet, that was A LOT.

THE SEVERITY OF THE TEST

Rebekah could have backed off from her commitment, and no one would have blamed her!

A camel can easily drink up to forty gallons of water at a time, and there were ten camels with Eleazar, so that means this particular group of camels could drink four hundred gallons of water. When it dawned on Rebekah what a massive task she had undertaken, she could have backed off from her commitment, and no one would have blamed her.

These camels had traveled some five hundred miles, and they were very thirsty. They would take her back those five hundred miles to her destiny, but she didn't know that yet. As she gave them water to drink, she was unknowingly preparing them for the return journey and, unknowingly, securing her own future. This is a truth that should bless us all: by serving others well, you are actually serving yourself.

Looking at Genesis 24 from the natural point of view,

it is amazing just how important a part these seemingly insignificant camels played. Here, in this chapter, we find the great Abraham, Isaac, Rebekah and Eleazar—all created in the image of God and all destined for greatness. But could any of it have happened without the participation of the camels? Looking at it from another perspective, we could say that the camels were the most important characters in the chapter.

It was the camels that presented Rebekah with the test and, thus, with an opportunity for the future. The season of your life when anything and everything seems to be unimportant could very well be the most important season for you. And if you miss the mark in this season, other opportunities may not come your way.

It's so easy to serve when important people are in the room or when those to be served are mighty men in our eyes. And it's so easy to let your guard down when no one of importance is present. The greatest mistakes can be made just at these moments. Rebekah was tested by ten unimpressive-looking camels.

Who would have thought that behind those camels was a setup? Who would have thought that on the backs of those camels were the gifts that would turn her life around? As we have noted, God loves to hide His greatest blessings in unimposing wrappings, and camels don't necessarily make the best wrapping paper in the world.

The camels that will irritate you and complicate your life will also become your ride to destiny, and ignoring the camels in life is to ignore your very future. Be careful, for your greatest blessing could be wrapped in a camel's coat. Your life connection will surely present itself, but you can take advantage of it only if and when you learn to serve in the unimportant things of life.

The things you serve that have no interest for you today will surely get all your attention tomorrow—once you have a better understanding of your own destiny and purpose in life. If Rebekah had a prophetic eye concerning her future, she would know that camels that seem unimportant today can become mounts for tomorrow's destiny. That thing that is so unimportant to your life today could very well become the substance of your life tomorrow.

When you experience difficulty in life, it often causes others to leave you. No man wants to participate in another man's problems. When you are left alone with your own difficulties, God will show up in your loneliness, and He will make sure you are the only recipient when it comes time for the rewards.

When it came time for the bride to be identified, Rebekah was the only choice. She alone was able to rejoice in the special gifts to be given to a special and unique woman because she alone had passed the test.

Although the frustrations in your life seem to serve no useful purpose, they just might carry things to your house that are desperately needed. Eleazar, as much as he might have liked to carry the special gifts to Rebekah, could not do it. Neither could the men who accompanied him. Only the pesky camels could carry so much. It's not something we like to hear, but many of the unwelcome visitors who come into our lives are there for a divine purpose. They carry hidden blessings for us.

VARIATIONS ON A TRUTH

As proof of what we're saying here about the importance of the camels, I want to share with you in these pages some powerful verses from the Word of God in several different translations. This is done so that some of the small variations of meaning can be explored. The verses in question are James 1:2-4, with particular emphasis on verse 2.

FROM THE NEW KING JAMES VERSION

The New King James Version, the one that we are using as the principle translation for this book, says it this way:

My brethren, count it all joy when you fall into various trials, knowing that the testing of your faith produces patience. But let patience have its perfect work, that you may be perfect and complete, lacking nothing.

James 1:2-4

FROM THE LIVING BIBLE

Now, here are the same verses from the Living Bible:

My brethren, count it all joy when you fall into various trials, knowing that the testing of your faith produces patience. But let patience have its perfect work, that you may be perfect and complete, lacking nothing.

James 1:2-4, LIV

The purpose of trials and tests is *"that you may be perfect and complete, lacking nothing."* Who is this written to? It's written to you and to me. It is clear from these verses that in order for God to get us to the place of being *"perfect and complete,"* He has chosen to use trials and tests. I know that's not a popular message, and I wish I could tell you something different, but I didn't write the Bible. I can only report what it says.

FROM THE BERKELEY TRANSLATION

Verse 2 is translated a little differently in the Berkeley version:

> *You must regard it as nothing but joy when you are involved in all kinds of trials.*   James 1:2, BRK

This translation teaches us that through every trial and test, we should think of nothing but joy. Trials, after all, are not forever. They last only for a season (usually a fairly short season), and their purpose is to determine our true character and whether or not we truly believe that there is more to come. The intended result is blessing for us.

"Regard it as nothing but joy." Nothing! This may be a tall order for some, but the encouraging thing is that God sees you at the place where you will live in extreme joy, once He is finished working on you, in you and through you. And you'll get there, if you just keep moving forward with joy.

FROM GOOD NEWS FOR MODERN MAN

Good News for Modern Man takes this a step further:

> *"Consider yourselves fortunate..."*
>
> James 1:2, GNMM

Can this be right? *Fortunate,* in this context, means "favorite." Is there something special about being chosen to undergo all sorts of trials? What is clear is that when any trial comes our way, God has a plan for it to work to our good. The intensity of the attacks launched against you is a barometer of the level of the blessing that God is preparing for you when the trial is ended. *"Fortunate"* people must first be tested. So, when trials come, it's a sure sign that you're on your way to becoming a *"fortunate"* person.

Too often, our reaction to the trials of life is very different. I know people who have thought they were cursed or that they had missed God because

> *In order for God to get us to the place of being "perfect and complete," He has chosen to use trials and tests!*

bad things were happening to them. Joseph went to a pit, then to a house of lies (Potiphar's house) and then to jail, and yet the Bible declares emphatically that God was with Him through it all:

> *The LORD was with Joseph, and he was a successful man; and he was in the house of his master the Egyptian [Potiphar]. And his master saw that the LORD was with him and that the LORD made all he did to prosper in his hand. So Joseph found favor in his sight, and served him. Then he made him overseer of his house, and all that he had he put under his authority. So it was, from the time that he had made him overseer of his house and all that he had, that the LORD blessed the Egyptian's house for Joseph's sake; and the blessing of the LORD was on all that he had in the house and in the field. Thus he left all that he had in Joseph's hand, and he did not know what he had except for the bread which he ate.* Genesis 39:2-6

But no sooner had Joseph recovered from this tragedy than another one was upon him. His life seemed to be going from bad to worse. Still it is clear that the Lord was with him:

> *And Joseph's master took him, and put him into the prison, a place where the king's prisoners were bound: and he was there in the prison. But the LORD was with Joseph, and showed him mercy, and gave him favour*

*in the sight of the keeper of the prison. And the keeper
of the prison committed to Joseph's hand all the pris-
oners that were in the prison; and whatsoever they
did there, he was the doer of it. The keeper of the prison
looked not to any thing that was under his hand; because the LORD was with him, and that which he did,
the LORD made it to prosper.* Genesis 39:20-23, KJV

God had a purpose in all of this, and these experiences, rather than defeat Joseph, only lifted him higher.
Never allow circumstances to lie to you and tell you that
you have missed God. He is in every situation that you
face in your daily life. Instead of exhibiting doubts and
disappointment, *"consider yourself fortunate."*

FROM THE NEW ENGLISH BIBLE

The New English Bible says it this way:

*Whenever you have to face trials of many kinds count
yourself supremely happy.*   James 1:2, NEB

Happiness, according to this translation, can come to
us through trials. Why? Because those who are tested and
proven worthy are destined for promotion. You are in the
class of supreme happiness because the Lord knows something about your future that you don't yet know.

We are *"fortunate"* to be going through so much, and
we should be *"supremely happy"* about it. Mere happiness
is not good enough. God wants us to be *"supremely happy,"*

and He is ready to take us to a new level of joy because of what we endure. You never have to worry about going through trials and tests and then not enjoying the very same intensity of blessing to come. Every test carries with it potential blessings.

> **Even when the trials come as crowds, we should see them as "friends" and welcome their appearance!**

FROM THE J.B. PHILLIPS TRANSLATION

The J.B. Phillips translation of the New Testament says it this way:

When all kinds of trials and temptations crowd into your lives, my brothers, don't resent them as intruders, but welcome them as friends.

James 1:2, PHI

What kind of *"friends"* are these? This translation shows that *"trials and temptations"* will come to us in crowds. There will be many of them, and they will strike all at once. But even when the trials come as crowds, we should see them as *"friends"* and welcome their appearance.

Why? Friends do us good. They care for us as individuals. So the thing you thought would harm you is the very thing that will bless you. Blessings sometimes have a negative start, but they always have an incredible ending. What you now consider your enemy is actually your *"friend."* So, welcome it as such.

One thing is clear: God is about to turn things around for you. He is about to turn the tide in your life. So, cheer up, dear friend. Things will get better very soon. Serve your camels well, for they carry something you don't want to miss once they are unpacked, and they will be used to carry you to your destiny.

FROM THE MESSAGE

The *Message* uses these incredible words:

Throw yourselves a party.   James 1:2, MES

Just how far can we go with this truth? Is this some kind of printer's error, perhaps? Not at all. This is exactly what the Bible says. We are to welcome problems as *"friends,"* knowing that there is some hidden blessing in them for us. And we are to go so far as to *"throw [ourselves] a party"* to celebrate the privilege of facing such trials and tests, the privilege of being favored in this way.

Does that make sense? Why would God want us to celebrate such things? Because He sees beyond what we can see. He knows the end from the beginning. He wants to bring our eventual celebration out of the future and into the present.

Again, our trials, tests and temptations are not forever,

and therefore we are encouraged to see them in a positive light. If God allows them to come to us, He must know that we can stand the test and move on to greater things. So, go ahead. *"Throw [yourself] a party."*

TESTS ARE UNIVERSAL

EVERY MAN AND WOMAN OF GOD FACES TESTS

Every man and woman of God faces tests, and how they face them determines the outcome. When David fought against Goliath, I believe he envisioned himself married to the king's daughter. In order to marry her, he would have to face the giant and kill him, and he was able to face the giant because of his hope of a better tomorrow.

Your resistance is the very thing that will take you to your destiny, and your gateway to the bride is the particular giant you're facing even now. Your enemy is just a formality on the way to your reward. If God has already given you a description of the reward, then why should resistance concern you at all?

God told Joshua:

See! I have given Jericho into your hand, its king, and the mighty men of valor.   Joshua 6:2

Between Joshua and this promise stood the walls of Jericho, but God gave him a strategy for making those walls come down. The enemies of the Israelites were driven back because of their fear of the people of God, and they took cover behind the walls of the city. The fact that your enemies seem to be secure behind some walls doesn't mean that they're invincible. The walls of that city do not represent resistance. They're just the method God uses to assemble your enemies for easy defeat.

If God says, "I have given you the city," then you have two choices: You can look at the walls and be dismayed, or you can look at God's promise and rejoice. David saw the giant before him, but he chose, instead, to focus on the reward. In the same way, if we know that there's a reward coming to us from Christ, then the battle we must face in the meantime is little more than a formality.

If your current trial is only a formality, and your current test will only last for a season, you have reason to celebrate. Go ahead, *"throw yourself a party."*

Without the pit, Joseph could not have received the palace. Yes, he had other trials as well. The wife of a powerful official (Potiphar) lied about him, saying that he had tried to molest her. That was a very serious charge, and how can you defend yourself against lies? How can you control everything that others choose to say about you? Anybody can make up whatever they want to, and often it will be believed before the truth. But Joseph had to be lied about so that he could be promoted.

Why did he then have to go to jail? Weren't the pit and the lies enough? Now came a third bad season of his life, and Joseph must have begun to wonder if his dreams were really from God and if they would ever come true.

Every single one of us must endure enough trials to know that we've had reason to give up. But beyond the pit, the lies and the jail, there was a palace waiting. Beyond your greatest test, your breakthrough is waiting. With the same intensity with which people lie about you today, they will tell the truth about you in the future. So don't worry about their lies. When we stay on track for what the Lord has for us, He will make sure that our interests are taken care of.

EVEN JESUS HAD TO BE TESTED

The Word of God teaches that it was the Holy Spirit who led Jesus into the desert to be tempted, or tested:

> *Then Jesus was led up by the Spirit into the wilderness to be tempted by the devil.*   Matthew 4:1

Jesus was not drawn into the desert by the devil, and desert experiences do not always come from the evil one. Jesus had to be in that desert, and He had to face the devil there. He was led there *"by ... the Spirit."* But He also came forth from that experience in the power of the Spirit, and when He did, there was a whole new dynamic to His life and ministry. During that desert experience, He was empowered, and He came out of the experience more powerful than when He went in.

In the context of this truth, we can see that you and I need our challenges in order to develop. It is the challenge that will reveal our weaknesses and will give us an opportunity to grow in the area where we need it the most.

The most precious diamonds and gold come from deep under the earth, and it costs millions of dollars to get them out. But, although millions are spent to get those materials out, that's nothing in comparison to the trillions of dollars that will be generated through their sale. Serve God in excellence, for a precious, as yet untold, gift has your name on it and is, even now, coming your way.

Your reward is closer than you think. Rebekah was never far away from hers. She served the camels, not realizing that her fortune and destiny were within her reach. She was just one camel ride away from her covenant dream.

God hides His treasures where no one expects them to be. He keeps them where no man can get to them. What would be the use of a gift that is easily available? God's greatest gifts were designed to be

> *The most precious diamonds and gold come from deep under the earth, and it costs millions of dollars to get them out!*

discovered through the spirit of servanthood. Therefore, proud, arrogant and stubborn people will never find these gifts. Only those who have the spirit of a servant will discover God's greatest blessings.

PRIDE IS THE ENEMY OF SERVANTHOOD

TRUE SERVANTHOOD PRECLUDES PRIDE AND ARROGANCE

A true servant is one who serves where arrogance and pride would never be found, and a true servant is always closer to the blessing than an arrogant and prideful person could ever hope to be. The Bible is full of this truth:

The one who has a haughty look and a proud heart,
Him I will not endure.   Psalm 101:5

Pride and arrogance and the evil way
And the perverse mouth I hate.   Proverbs 8:13

Pride goes before destruction,
And a haughty spirit before a fall.   Proverbs 16:18

When everyone (including the prophet Samuel) thought that Eliab or one of his other mature brothers would be the next king of Israel, God chose, instead, a shepherd boy. His name was David. Eliab, who was the oldest brother in the family, did not understand that. Why would the youngest, most inexperienced of the boys, be appointed? When Samuel arrived, Eliab and his other brothers were in the house, but David wasn't even there. He was out serving the sheep. Good shepherds love to serve sheep, because they know that sheep are helpless creatures that cannot think for themselves.

When God told Samuel that Eliab was not the one (and the same with his other brothers), Samuel asked if there might be another son. Jesse admitted that there was one more, and David was sent for. (If you serve well, you may even be appointed in your absence.) Now, everything stopped while they all waited for David to come.

When the lad entered the room, Samuel immediately knew that he was the one, and he anointed him. David had only sheep experience and had not been considered a serious candidate to become king, but he was appointed because of his faithful service. A person who has the heart of a servant cannot be overlooked—even in his absence.

Often, strife, manipulation, trickery or connections are used to gain someone a position, but these tactics can only take you so far. God's man will always be appointed by divine intervention.

THE FOUR LEPROUS MEN

When God needed to save a nation from famine, He chose to bring the answer through four leprous men (see 2 Kings 6-7). The famine had gone on for so long that there was now no food to be found, and people were starving to death. God gave a word through His prophet that the next day, at about the very same time, there would be food in the gates of Samaria. And who was it who made the discovery the next day that saved the nation? It was the four lepers. Why? Because God hides His secrets in places where we never expect to find them. He doesn't do things in the same way a man would.

Leprosy is a terrible disease, one that degrades the physical body to the point that it is literally falling apart. Even in a spiritual sense, God sometimes takes people who seem to be literally falling apart, and He then makes them instruments for His glory. How great is His mercy!

> *God sometimes takes people who seem to be literally falling apart, and He then makes them instruments for His glory!*

Are you at the point of giving up? Are you perhaps contemplating disappearing from the scene and never coming back? Have you ever considered the thought that you could be God's next answer for humanity, and that multitudes might find Christ through you? Don't give up now. Your time has come. God is looking for humble servants.

A Boy, Five Loaves of Bread and Two Fish

When Jesus fed those four thousand men and their families, He chose to do it with the lunch of a little boy. It consisted of five loaves of bread and two fish. The disciples had thought it was time to send the people away, but Jesus told them to seat the people and serve them.

When the people were seated, it could then be seen what an enormous crowd it was. Have you seen what a crowd of twenty thousand people looks like? But the Man behind the five loaves and two fish was Jesus, and He is with you too. He is with you in your particular challenge—as great as it might seem. He is just waiting for you to serve.

Never ignore your challenge. Never look down on your fish and bread. Never treat your leprosy as if there were no purpose left for you to serve. If God is calling you, rise to the challenge. He is ready to exalt humble servants.

When the disciples, who should have known better, became so arrogant as to tell Jesus to send the people away, He used the insignificant lunch of an insignificant boy to prove them wrong. He hid His bakery and His fishery in the hands of a child, and you could be next.

That Humble Barn

As we have seen, when the living God sought a place for the birth of His Son, He chose a barn. Why a barn?

There were many reasons (and most of them are still undiscovered). One reason we know for sure: The greatest enemy of Jesus' birth was the devil, and if he had been able to locate the Child, he would have killed Him for sure. So God the Father allowed the King of kings and Lord of lords to be born in a place of obscurity, a place where no one would expect Him to be born. He didn't need to be born in a place of significance, because He is significance Himself. The place never makes the person; rather, the person makes the place.

Many need titles to make them look better, and thank God for titles, but let the gift tell who you are. Many times, a person's business card is more impressive than their ministry. Let God demonstrate the gift that He hides in you, and once the gift is in operation, we (the rest of the Body of Christ) will tell you who you are.

Please don't misunderstand what I'm saying here. I have many friends who have excelled in life, and we honor them. I will be the first in line to honor people who have great enthusiasm. The most important thing, however, will always be the substance that resides in us. Let that be uppermost.

But, returning to the point at hand, God chose a humble stable as the backdrop for this divine drama. Your house could be next.

That Humble Upper Room

When the Lord wanted to start His Church, He chose an upper room—not a hotel or the home of some important person. His greatness is in Himself, and He doesn't need a great place, a great name or the fame of another to make a statement. The place, the nature of the surroundings or who knows about it is not of any importance at all. His presence makes a place look great. He makes a statement wherever He is at the moment. He is the statement. Let Him use you where you are today.

God's Hidden Resources

God hides His prophets in the houses of widows, and He feeds His prophets through ravens. He hides His taxes in the mouth of a fish. He has absolutely incredible hiding places, and He chooses to reveal His glory from obscurity.

Gideon's three hundred men were identified by the way they drink water. They were the minority, and they were also the ones through whom God brought forth victory.

The children of Israel had to walk around the city of Jericho for seven days. After seven days, when it began to look as though they were being humiliated, it became clear that God hides Himself in the silence of obedience.

When praise from the mouth of Paul and Silas seemed irrelevant (in the light of their situation in jail in Philippi), God revealed Himself as the Deliverer. Let Him show Himself strong on your behalf today.

Leah was unloved by Jacob, and yet she was the hiding place for six of the future twelve tribes of Israel. She was the wife who gave birth to Judah, the son who's name meant "praise." It was from the line of Leah that David, the greatest king in the Old Testament, was born. And to crown it all, Jesus, the Christ, came forth out of her lineage as well.

When an insignificant bush would not stop burning, Moses realized that God was in it. He hides Himself among the lions, where fearful humans would never go. Daniel discovered that it's possible to be protected even among such ferocious beasts. There, in the midst of his current circumstances, he found God hiding Himself.

In Egypt, God hid His power in an old, dry stick. Then, when Moses and Aaron faced Pharaoh, God revealed Himself through that stick. The two brothers probably looked very insignificant that day standing in the splendor of Egypt. They may well have seemed totally unprofessional, but when it came time for action, God revealed Himself again, and He did it from obscurity.

In the little jar of the Shunamite women, God hid His multiplying ability and brought forth that oil refinery. The very jar that had represented her insufficiency (and perhaps she had even forgotten about it or cast it aside) became the hiding place from which God would initiate her greatest miracle, a miracle that would calm all her fears.

As the head of the Syrian army, Naaman was a very important person, but he was a leper. When fear struck him and he tried to run to the king and even impress him with gold, silver and clothing, a little girl referred him to the prophet Elisha. Naaman was totally outside of his comfort zone and his understanding, but God worked a miracle and healed him from leprosy. He found God hiding Himself in the little girl who was responsible for directing this important man to someone with power from on high.

Again, God used those four leprous men. They had been thrown out, because they posed a health threat to the city. But while the rest of the nation was dying, they were the ones to discover the fact that their enemies had fled. They could have kept the news (and the spoils) to themselves, but they made it known, and the nation was saved.

Was it just another coincidence that four lepers were the ones who made that wonderful discovery? Not at all. It was not by chance that they saved the nation from starvation. Once again, it was with the unexpected, the unprecedented and the rejected that God

The four lepers could have kept the news (and the spoils) to themselves, but they made it known, and the nation was saved!

hid His insight, knowledge and supply. And He is ready to use you today.

In Jesus' time, God hid Himself in a storm at sea. The disciples were in the boat on that sea, and early in the morning they saw someone walking toward them. They thought it was a ghost (It was at the time of morning when demons are most active), but it was Jesus—when and where they least expected Him. They had expected their lives to be lost because of the storm, but He rides on the storm and turns what you thought was death into life. God will show up at your darkest hour, walking on the water.

Whatever the circumstances of your life today—even if those circumstances seem to be the most insignificant, the most tragic or the most unfair—God is ready to give you great victory through them. So, go ahead. *"Throw [yourself] a party."* You have something to celebrate.

CHAPTER 6

BY A WELL OF WATER

And he made his camels kneel down outside the city by a well of water at evening time, the time when women go out to draw water. Genesis 24:11

I love this phrase, *"the time when women go out to draw water."* We are living in a time when the human race is seeking something that can quench the thirsting of their souls. Man was created in the image of God and has within him (or her) a deep desire for the supernatural. A man may run from God, but deep inside he has a desire to live in His presence.

Water that can quench our thirst is something that cannot be ignored by anyone, and so it's time to draw. It's time to get more of God, time to go and find the place where water flows in abundance. Let us call all the nations, all the tribes and all the various colors of humanity. Let us go to the Living Well and draw water that will quench our thirst.

There is no such thing as Assembly of God water, Presbyterian water or Independent water. God Himself is the Well. He is the Source for all humanity, and the time has come for people from all walks of life to start drinking from Him.

THE TIMING OF ELEAZAR'S VISIT

Eleazar made sure that he was at the well by the time the women came out to draw water. He knew what that time was, and he used that information to his advantage. In the same way, God's Spirit, knowing the human race, has made a plan to be where He needs to be in order to make contact with those who seek water in this hour.

In Eleazar's case, it was evening, and darkness was quickly approaching. God's Spirit will encounter the human race in darkness. Without God, we're all in the evening of our lives, and we're fast approaching the darkest night the human race has ever faced, the night of sin.

"The time when women go out to draw water" was a time when nothing else could be allowed to be more important. Water, in itself, is life, and Jesus is referred to in the Scriptures as *"the water of life"*:

> *And the Spirit and the bride say, "Come!" And let him who hears say, "Come!" And let him who thirsts come. Whoever desires, let him take the water of life freely.*
>
> Revelation 22:17

When the time for drawing water had come, no man could be allowed to stop it. Water was essential, and it still is. The human race has no option but to stop and seek the water it needs. It is impossible to ignore water without dying. The greatest atheist can never exist in the natural without water. How can such a person even try to assume that there is no God in Heaven, when He is *"the Water of Life"*?

God, our heavenly Father, knew that, and He made a plan called the salvation plan. He sent Jesus to the earth at just the right time. He was waiting for you and me to become thirsty, and when we appeared, He was there to present Himself to us for an eternal connection.

At the evening time, before we entered the darkness of night, we found Jesus. At the well of much water, we found the water that quenches our thirst, and the connection between the human race and God, the Creator of all life, was made for eternity.

> *When the time for drawing water had come, no man could be allowed to stop it!*

ELEAZAR WAS POSITIONED AT THE WELL

Eleazar positioned himself at the well where the women normally came to draw water. It was the logical place. Why would a man look elsewhere? Why would God send His Son to other planets, if He knew He had placed man on Earth?

These are the days when the Holy Spirit will position Himself at the wells of life, and there He will stand to offer us water to drink. Once we drink from that well, we will never need to draw water again, for we will have a fountain of living water coming forth from within us.

God knows your movements. He knows that you will become thirsty and will have no option but to visit the well. He knows that you will come, and therefore all He needs to do is to position Himself and wait for you.

Jesus positioned Himself at the cross years before you were even born, and He's waiting for us to visit that cross so we can receive what we so desperately need.

Again, the time when the women drew water was in the evening, and evening suggests a lateness. It suggests that it was getting dark. There was not much time left in the day.

Evening is when light fades into darkness, and we are now living in the last days. It is the evening of time. Now is the moment for the Holy Spirit to position Himself in order to find a Bride, and He knows the perfect place to find her—at the well.

As we approach the well and begin to draw water, you and I may not even be expecting anything to happen. Still, as we go about the normal activities of our day, we will find that God's Spirit, by grace, has positioned Himself. He's waiting for us. The end result will be that we walk right into the incredible blessings that are there waiting for us.

Why will this happen? Because of the desire in the heart of God, the Father. There was a desire in the heart of Abraham to find a bride for his son, and that desire drove Eleazar forward, even though Rebekah didn't even know Abraham. Our heavenly Father has had a desire to make us part of the Bride for His Son—without us even knowing about it. This is better known as the "Salvation Plan of God." Thank God He included us.

What we have here in Genesis 24 is a prophetic picture of the salvation plan of God for the end time. The Holy Spirit is positioning Himself at the wells of life. There, where we go to seek life (represented by the water), He is ready to offer us eternal life and take us on an eternal journey toward our destiny in eternity. The order that we must follow to achieve this goal is first preparation, then positioning and, finally, possession.

PREPARATION, POSITIONING AND POSSESSION

PREPARATION

In order to know how to run a particular race, many similar races must first be run. Any athlete who competes professionally has already run many other unofficial races before the one that counts is scheduled. The race that counts, of course, is the one that will be run before

> *In order to run a legal race and not face disqualification, you must learn ahead of time to do what will later be expected of you!*

thousands of people. At that point, television cameras will surely be focused on you. In order to position yourself for such a race, you need to gain knowledge of how that race needs to be run.

Unless and until you have run many races, you will never be able to run the race that counts. In order to run the race that counts, you need to run that same race again and again in a place where no one is watching you and where you can make mistakes, and they will not be counted against you. In order to run a legal race and not face disqualification, you must learn ahead of time to do what will later be expected of you.

Any athlete who runs the one-hundred-meter dash in the Olympics and wins will admit this fact. He has run that same race dozens of times before. He has done it over and over and over again, and winning now is just a repetition of what he has already done many times before. Winning requires preparation and lots of it.

Many people don't like preparation. Preparation is a place and/or a situation in which you will practice your dream over and over again, until you are ready to do it before a crowd. If you don't practice where the crowd can't distract you, you'll never be able to focus on your vision when a crowd is shouting at you. If you cannot win where there is no honor, once honor comes (along with the large crowds), it will destroy you. If you only want to run where there is a crowd to witness it, and you cannot run well where there is no crowd, it's a sign that you're all about the crowd and not about the vision.

The greatest test for those who serve is to do it when no one it watching and still insist on doing it well. The question was once asked to a man of God who has a very big television ministry today: "What do you do differently now that you have success?" His answer was enlightening: "I'm still doing today what I was doing all the years of my life, before anyone knew about me." That is a very powerful key to success.

Preparation, or positioning yourself, for possessing your destiny will require that you serve faithfully where you are and that you keep on doing the thing you believe you were called to do in life. Someday, when you are in your destiny, you'll still do what you do today, but you'll do it without most of the mistakes you're still making now. The great difference will be that you'll be in the public eye, where you cannot afford to make such mistakes, and that is why preparation without a crowd is so important.

A good speaker becomes a good speaker by speaking, believing that the more he uses the gift, the better the gift will become. A jockey practices riding alone, and he does it over and over again. He is motivated by the belief that doing this will eventually bring him to the ultimate race of his life. If you are not faithful in your preparation, where no one can see you, you will never be chosen to do what you've done all the years of your life before other people.

Rebekah was not coming to the well for the first time that day. She must have drawn hundreds of pitchers full of water before. She was accustomed to this service. The only difference this time was that she had become so good at it that she had the boldness to offer her services to a foreigner and to his camels. Unless you use your gift when you are alone, you will never have the boldness to use it in the presence of other people. It's preparation that leads to positioning.

POSITIONING

Eleazar positioned himself at the well, but Rebekah had to be there too. A crowd of people attending a race will never have the chance to see a certain runner perform unless he has first positioned himself for the race through preparation. Only those who have prepared themselves while remaining unseen will ever be allowed to position themselves before the crowd. If you cannot inspire yourself to run a race in which no one sees the result and it's all about exercise and personal training, you will never be allowed to run in public. If you have not prepared for the race when no one can see you, you will not qualify to run the race where people can see you. Trying to position yourself for a race that you have never trained for in private can prove to be very humiliating.

The very act of positioning yourself for a race says a lot about you. It says that you have been in this thing for many years, and you have done what was needed for your preparation. It is your preparation that has brought you to the day of positioning. Many people want to be great without first being tested. If you expect to one day run in the Olympics (where millions of people can watch you), you must first be willing to run an Olympic race in which no one is watching, and to do that over and over for many years.

When Eleazar positioned himself at the well that day, it was a well-thought-through act. He must have taken his camels to many wells before this, but this time was different. This was a setup with a divine purpose, and Eleazar knew that this act could trigger something incredible. It was at the well that he would find the desired bride for Isaac. It was at the well where Rebekah would come to draw water.

Because she was there too, it was there, at the well of positioning, that Eleazar saw Rebekah. And when your season for recognition comes, God will have the Holy

Spirit ready to recognize you. You will perform the required act of obedience that day, and it will catch the eye of the Spirit.

Eleazar positioned himself at the well so that he could find Rebekah, and I believe that now, more than ever, the Holy Spirit is positioning Himself at the wells of life to find the Rebekahs who are ready to serve. Keep on serving as Rebekah did, because you never know who might be positioned at your well to observe.

The important thing is to stay humble once you have been discovered. When he was still very young, Joseph received a dream from God that he would become the Prime Minister. That dream puffed him up to the point that he had to go through three negative seasons in order for God to remove the spirit of pride from his life. He went to the pit, to Potiphar's house and then to prison. If just a dream can make a person that prideful, can you imagine how dangerous it is when the fulfillment of the dream comes, and it suddenly becomes a reality in your life? The very thing that should bless you can very easily become your destruction. If you're not a willing servant at your well, you won't be able to remain a servant in the fulfillment of your dream. Before you can serve your Isaac, you will be asked to serve at the well many times.

It is no wonder, then, that God gave Rebekah ten camels to water. It is the unimportant things in life that will bring out the real you. If one frustration in life were not enough, how about ten? It is the multiplication of frustrations in our lives that God uses to make sure we're set free (or if we need more deliverance). Possession can never come (and will never come) unless and until you have faithfully and consistently served at your well. Prepare and then position yourself.

POSSESSION

Prophetically, Eleazar was a picture of how the Holy Spirit positions Himself at the wells of life to attract the Church. Once the Church serves well, it is the Spirit's intention to take us on a journey to meet the Bridegroom in the air and to prepare us, the Church, to spend eternity with Christ.

> *The important thing is to stay humble once you have been discovered!*

To possess, you must take a different approach than the person who simply positions himself at the well. For our purposes, the well here speaks of the local church, and many people need to position themselves there. It is through faithful service at the well that they will ultimately take possession of what belongs to them. Is your local church just a place you visit sometimes, or are you playing a major role at the well? Rebekah played a major role at her well, and through that faithful service, she become a possessor.

Eleazar knew the custom of the women to visit the

well and draw water, and he knew that he could find water there as well. More importantly, he knew that he could find a suitable bride there. There are certain places the Holy Spirit expects us to be. Are we frequenting the places He will search for us? Or do we find ourselves "too busy" with other things to be where He is stationed?

Are we busy doing what we are called to do? Are we drawing water on a regular basis, so that we can then touch others with the commodity God's Spirit will require of us? Or will He find us with something else in our hands? An even more important question would be this: Will He find the attitude of serving being demonstrated in us when He comes?

Apart from having access to water and knowing how to draw water, Rebekah was qualified to become the bride because she had the attitude of a servant. It was not the water that qualified her; it was the spirit of a servant. Water may well be the most needed substance for life, but without a servant to bring it to them, many would surely die. Rebekah could have insisted upon concentrating on drawing water for her personal needs, but, instead, she chose to think of and minister to the needs of others.

Considering that the well can be seen as a type of the local church, are we attending church just for ourselves? Or do we fill up for the purpose of serving others?

Imagine what it would have been like for Eleazar if he had not been able to find Rebekah at the well. Be at the place you need to be, for the Holy Spirit will not seek to find you at any other place. Serve where God has positioned you. If you are not humble enough to serve at the place of your appointment, you will ultimately miss your destiny.

Promotion Comes Out of Humility

Rebekah's promotion came out of her humble spirit. God never exalts prideful people.

You may run fast trying to find destiny, not realizing that your destiny is within you. The rudder that will steer you to the destiny in your life is already in you. If you are faithful to listen to that voice inside you, you will constantly be moving closer to your destiny.

God is drawn toward faithfulness, and faithfulness will eventually take you to greatness. Greatness is not to be found in the places a man can take you or what a man can do for you; greatness is found in you having and displaying the spirit of a servant.

Jesus knew all the right people, but what made Him who He was was the meek and humble Spirit that was in Him. He was, He said, sent to the poor:

> *The Spirit of the Lord God is upon Me,*
> *Because the Lord has anointed Me*
> *To preach good tidings to the poor.*   Isaiah 61:1

Jesus' humility made Him great in due season. He served people who could not reward Him. He who does not want to be humble has no chance for greatness, for greatness is to be found in humility. Humility means that you are not constantly thinking of yourself, but of your service to others. Humble people don't even know that they're humble. It comes naturally to them.

Are you properly positioned at the well, humbly serving to draw the Spirit's attention? Like it or not, that is what's required.

CHAPTER 7

BEHOLD, I STAND HERE

Behold, I stand here by the well of water, and the daughters of the men of the city are coming out to draw water.

Genesis 24:13

Eleazar was positioned for success, and there he waited until it came his way. Never despise the place of your positioning. God positioned Nehemiah to see the walls of Jerusalem broken down. He always finds someone who will take responsibility for what needs to be done.

Rebekah, too, was positioned. She was being set up for serving, so that she could capture her destiny. In the challenge, you will always find your destiny.

THE ROAD TO DESTINY ALWAYS RUNS THROUGH SOME CHALLENGE

The road to destiny always runs through some challenge, and to refuse a challenge is to ignore destiny. People of destiny are people who are involved in a challenge of some kind. Destiny seekers will constantly face challenges.

Any destiny found will be found on the other side of your challenge.

Beyond the cross of Jesus, eternity waited. Beyond his pain, suffering and humiliation, salvation, healing and deliverance waited. Many people say they don't like change, but to say no to change is to say no to a challenge. To say no to both change and challenge is to say no to progress.

Progress can never be achieved without change or challenge!

Progress can never be achieved without change or challenge. If there isn't any challenge, you can never accomplish anything of significance, and if you fail to accomplish anything of significance in life, you will never taste satisfaction. That would leave you with a very unimpressive and boring life. You'd be going nowhere.

Nehemiah met his challenge, when he saw that the walls of Jerusalem were broken down. In receiving this challenge (and the accompanying responsibilities), he walked right into his destiny. Destiny for him started with the news of burned-down walls. David's destiny started with the news of a vulgar giant. Hannah's destiny started with barrenness, and Jesus' greatest accomplishment started with that despised cross.

Joseph's palace experience started with him being thrown into a pit. Joshua's conquest of the Promised Land started by him realizing that Moses was dead and that he could no longer depend upon the infrastructure of the past.

Many think that destiny is a place where nothing goes wrong, everything goes right, and things just seem to fall into place. But destiny can never be found unless and until the challenge at hand has been met, and the moment the promise of destiny falls on you, challenges of every sort will soon follow.

WHAT IS DESTINY?

My own humble perception of destiny, in the light of the experiences I've had, is this: Destiny is a place you arrive at, having godly dreams for your life fulfilled. It is a place you arrive at, after having to go through many challenges and trials. You arrive at destiny in the season of your life when you can announce, like the apostle Paul:

> *As for me, my life has already been poured out as an offering to God. The time of my death is near. I have fought a good fight, I have finished the race, and I have remained faithful. And now the prize awaits me—the crown of righteousness that the Lord, the righteous Judge, will give me on that great day of his return. And the prize is not just for me but for all who eagerly look forward to his glorious return.* 2 Timothy 4:6-8, NLT

Paul had accomplished what pleased God, fulfilling God's dreams for his life, not his own. Therefore, destiny is the place of satisfaction, where one can say, "I have been obedient to the voice of God." It is to arrive at the place He desires for your life, as much as it is to be fulfilled as an individual. Destiny is to be in the perfect will of God for your life, with the emphasis on His dream for you. It is the completion of His utmost dream for your life, a place of knowledge and deep conviction where you have arrived at God's desire.

Destiny can only be found on the other side of a sacrifice. It is that place of deep inward satisfaction that no man, church or even a mentor can ever give you, that place where flesh will acknowledge that any accomplishment finally comes because of God's grace and mercy. It is a place of utmost peace, filled with a deep sense of inward satisfaction that you have just arrived at the perfect place, the place called the will of God for your life.

Insisting on only fulfilling your own desires will leave you with a feeling of incompleteness. Arriving at your destiny will make you a person who knows he has accomplished the highest calling in life, namely, to do the will of God.

Destiny is to accomplish, arrive at and step into the manifested, tailor-made design God has for your life. It is the reward God gives to those who are obedient, the thing you were created for. It is that place of utmost joy and satisfaction that you need to run to—no matter what the cost.

GOD POSITIONED EZEKIEL IN THE VALLEY OF DRY BONES

Ezekiel was destined by God to become a prophet who would turn a curse into a blessing, but God set him down in a valley full of dry bones and then asked him the question, *"Can these bones live?"* (Ezekiel 37:3). That was his challenge. In order to taste destiny, you'll have to accept the particular challenge set before you. It is the challenge that will take you to your destiny.

Ezekiel was transported to the valley of dry bones by the hand of God, but the way out of the valley was very different. The only way Ezekiel could get out was by accepting God's challenge. And what was that challenge? God expected Ezekiel to prophesy life to those dry bones.

To prophesy means to bring God's viewpoint to earthly matters. So, in order for Ezekiel to get out, he had to prophesy his way out. By doing that, he not only became the instrument used to deliver thousands of people, but he also received the victorious taste of destiny. The dry bones that were such a challenge were also his gateway to destiny. And your greatest enemy might just become your gateway to your greatest accomplishments.

GOD POSITIONED PAUL AND SILAS IN A JAIL

What made Paul and Silas such impressive people? As we read about them, we note their impressive ministries, and we are in awe of how the Lord used them. But not every day was one of victory for these two men. In Philippi, we see them in jail, and that was a difficult trial.

What made that particular jail so memorable? It was the way they came out of it.

They approached their experience in jail by singing songs of praise, when none of the other inmates felt much like singing. At what should have been their greatest time of discouragement, they sang:

> *But at midnight Paul and Silas were praying and singing hymns to God, and the prisoners were listening to them. Suddenly there was a great earthquake, so that the foundations of the prison were shaken; and immediately all the doors were opened and everyone's chains were loosed.*   Acts 16:25-26

What made these men leaders of the Church and men of destiny? They accepted the challenge of their trial and sang in the face of difficulty. That allowed them to walk into their destiny. It was that jail that helped them on their way to greatness.

Difficult circumstances, tests and trials are the breeding ground for songs of deliverance. Your camel of frustration is the gateway to something being birthed in your spirit so that you can glorify God even more.

Isaiah wrote:

> *"Sing, 0 barren,*
> *You who have not borne!*
> *Break forth into singing, and cry aloud,*
> *You who have not labored with child!*

For more are the children of the desolate
Than the children of the married women," says the
Lord.   Isaiah 54:1

A song of deliverance is never a song of deliverance unless it can deliver you. A song of deliverance is birthed in your spirit while you are still in bondage. Singing in the face of adversity proves the power of praise and its effectiveness. The way out, once again, was not by ignoring the challenge, but, rather, by joyfully accepting it. Sing while you are barren, for it is the barren who are instructed to sing. Why? Because negative circumstances are the breeding ground for the best praise ever heard.

A song of deliverance is never a song of deliverance unless it can deliver you!

GOD POSITIONED JOHN ON THE BARREN ISLE OF PATMOS

The island known as Patmos was said to be a barren place, with few trees or other vegetation. The ground was covered with stones. What a difficult place to be! But that's exactly where the apostle John was exiled. Why, then, do we think of him as a man of purpose and destiny? When he landed in this, the most difficult place we might imagine, he proceeded to receive a visitation from the Lord. This visitation changed him, and he wrote down what the Lord was showing him. The writing that resulted became known as the book of Revelation, an important part of our New Testament, and, through it, God has touched many generations.

John is known as a man of destiny because he accepted the challenge. Sometimes God must separate us from others so that He can work things out of us. Many of the letters of the apostle Paul that we enjoy reading and reciting today were written while he was in various prisons. The impressive vision John received came to him among the stones of Patmos in the heat of the day. His negative circumstances became his platform from which he ministered to the world, and from which he was launched into his own personal destiny.

GOD POSITIONED CALEB AMONG UNFRIENDLY GIANTS

Caleb is referred to in the Bible as a man with *"a different spirit"* (Numbers 14:24). When his brothers saw giants, he saw grapes. There were giants, but there were also grapes. Caleb wasn't blind. He, too, saw giants. But when he chose to report to Moses that he had seen grapes, he had decided in his heart that he would deal with the giants later. He reported to Moses that the land could be taken.

People who become known as people of destiny are those who have decided that resistance is just a bridge they need to walk over in order to end up in their destiny. People of destiny ignore the bad and focus on the good. The *"different spirit"* that Caleb carried was revealed in the midst of giants. The real you can only be revealed in the midst of a challenge, and the character of a man is revealed by what it takes to stop him.

Because his spirit was so different, Caleb saw a future for himself in the midst of those giants. In fact, he claimed the mountains where those very giants lived as his own and was willing to fight them to possess it. People of destiny, even in the fulfillment of their destiny, choose to live in the midst of some challenge, some giant, and they prefer to focus on grapes.

It was the giants, or challenges, that made Caleb feel that this was his place. Salt that remains in a salt shaker serves no purpose. Too many Christians seek the perfect place to live, a place where they won't have any challenge or resistance. Too late, they discover that their life has been wasted. A place such as they seek can only be found in Heaven. Get your eyes off of the challenge, and see the glorification of Jesus in and through your challenge.

The challenges you face in life reveal who you are. Character can only be seen in what it will take to stop you. Many people are forever talking about what they will do "when my ship comes in," how well they will run, when their season finally comes. In the meantime, they lose sight of the fact that before they can get a grip on their destiny they need to cross over the Jordan. They

> *In the natural, Rebekah's pitcher was much too small for this job, but the minute she accepted the challenge, she became a woman of destiny!*

have to get their own feet in the water. The water of the Jordan will never roll back until you first step into it. In order to walk through your problem, you need to stand in it.

GOD POSITIONED REBEKAH IN THE MIDST OF TEN THIRSTY CAMELS

In the natural, Rebekah's pitcher was much too small for this job, but the minute she accepted the challenge, she became a woman of destiny.

How could she fill the stomachs of ten camels (again, that was twenty big stomachs, because each camel had two of them)? Her pitcher was designed to draw water for a few people. What could she do?

Rebekah was destined for Isaac, but if she had failed to accept the challenge, she would never have become his wife. In losing Isaac, she would have lost much more than a husband. She would have lost her destiny. Ignoring your challenge is to ignore your Isaac, your destiny.

Many people cannot understand why they never find their destiny in life. They don't seem to have many problems, but neither are they extremely happy. As we have seen, James taught us to consider ourselves *"supremely happy"* when we suffer any sort of trial. When Rebekah said yes to her challenge, she was saying yes to her destiny and purpose.

ACCEPTING THE CHALLENGE

When we left our country of birth, South Africa, to come to America in January of 2001, Naomi, Amoré and I gave up many things that we had acquired over the years. This was our challenge: destiny or money. We could have stayed in South Africa, never paid the price that was being required of us and missed our destiny. But the taste of destiny is better than anything else we could ever imagine. We came to this country at the Lord's command, and we've never been sorry.

What if David had refused to fight the giant? For one thing, he would have lost the opportunity to marry the king's daughter. He also would have had to face that giant over and over again for the rest of his life. If not, the giant would have killed him.

In the end, God called David *"a man after His own heart"* (1 Samuel 13:14). David surely would never have received such a compliment from God if he had not been willing to face the giant. The giants you refuse to face today will hunt you down tomorrow and make your life miserable.

By fighting the giant, David accomplished another thing. He now had the knowledge that he could kill a giant. The knowledge of your previous accomplishments in the Lord will make the challenges of tomorrow so much easier.

While preaching in South Africa, the great German evangelist Reinhardt Bonnke once said that God moves with a man who moves. So, never get your eyes stuck on the size of your pitcher. Accept the challenge, and let the Lord increase the capacity of your gift.

The thing you refuse to fight and destroy will destroy you—if you do not first take off its head. Many people fail to accept their challenge, and, in the end, the challenge destroys them. Lose what you need to lose in order to get to the destiny of your life. Unless you accept your challenge and get it behind you, you will always dream about destiny, but you will never taste it.

When you dream about that destiny, in the season of living out your destiny, that dream will become an intense pain of "should have," "could have" and "would have." Certain risks are given by God as a challenge. Learn to face them squarely.

Your giant, the one you face today, is just a temporal obstacle. He cannot prevent you from achieving your purpose in life. David had in him the ability to overcome the giant, and he knew this even before he actually killed the Philistine. David's language, as he faced the giant, reflects the fact that he already saw the king's daughter becoming his wife.

If you are still dreaming of your destiny when in your old age, that may mean that you never killed your giant. But the challenge before you is the confirmation that something better is still waiting. The walls of Jericho with their sealed gates only confirmed that there was something more to believe for. The reason your enemy fights you is because he knows the value of what he's trying so desperately to keep from you. If he had nothing you needed to take from him, he wouldn't fight you so hard.

If the enemy is constantly coming against you, you can know that he's trying to keep you from something he knows belongs to you. He knows the Scriptures just as well as you do, and so he wants to resist you and to keep you from the things God has prepared for you.

Move On Toward Your Destiny

You have been positioned at the well for such a time as this. Once you taste destiny, it is the sign that your enemies are now positioned behind you and no longer in front of you. When this is true, it's not because of the success of his strategy, but because you have purposely put him there. When something is behind you, it indicates that you're moving on. So, keep moving forward.

In order to move a boat forward, you must put the oar in the water and use the force of the oar against the water to move the boat forward. That water can be a threat—if you look at it and think of the possibility of drowning. In the water, some die, but others use the very same water to move themselves forward.

An oar in the boat will take you nowhere. Get your oar of faith into the water, and use the water to move yourself forward. Resistance can become a tool for you to move forward into your destiny.

Are you facing some challenges today? If so, that's a good sign. You're moving in the right direction. Keep going, and you'll find your destiny.

CHAPTER 8

PLEASE GIVE ME SUCCESS THIS DAY

Then he said, "O Lord God of my master Abraham, please give me success this day, and show kindness to my master Abraham." Genesis 24:12

And he said, "Blessed be the Lord God of my master Abraham, who has not forsaken His mercy and His truth toward my master. As for me, being on the way, the Lord led me to the house of my master's brethren." Genesis 24:27

These words reveal Eleazar's innermost feelings. In his first prayer, he was asking God for success, success in finding the proper bride, success in fulfilling his master's commission. That bride would have the heart of a servant, to match the heart of the greatest servant who had ever lived—his master, Abraham. Clearly, the Church that will become Christ's Bride must be able to serve. She will have the heart of the greatest servant ever—Jesus.

When Eleazar had found Rebekah, he called his mission a success and gave thanks to God. What was it about Rebekah that made him feel that way?

SERVANTHOOD = SUCCESS

Most important of all, it was the spirit of servanthood that was on Rebekah, and this would prove to be her key to promotion. To serve means to carry the same Spirit that was in Jesus when He came to this earth. A prideful spirit simply cannot serve. In fact, to serve is the hardest thing anyone could ever ask of a prideful person. A prideful person may learn truths about serving and will make a mental note of them, but that's about as far as it goes.

A true servant, on the other hand, is not even aware of all that he has accomplished. He is only aware of the satisfaction he derives from serving. God will never promote arrogant and prideful people. In one sense, prideful people may get promoted, but usually only in their own eyes.

SERVICE IS EVERYTHING

Some years ago, Naomi and I took a trip on a cruise ship, and it gave us time to rest and also to write. During the cruise, I had the opportunity to speak with some of the workers on the ship. Some of them were waiters, others took care of the rooms and others performed other tasks. They all worked hard, months at a time, without a break. Watching them go about their daily duties, maintaining a pleasant attitude toward the passengers on the ship, I had to give them credit. They knew how to serve.

This intrigued me, and I wanted to get to the bottom of it. Whenever I asked any of them how they were doing, the answer was invariably the same: "Excellent sir." "But things can't be 'excellent' all the time," I insisted. Eventually one of the men opened his heart to me. "Sir," he confessed, "if I fail to answer 'excellent,' the captain will throw me off the ship." I had discovered the key. Excellence of service was one of the requirements of their work.

There were some three thousand passengers onboard that ship, and there were some nine hundred crew members to serve them. Written in various critical spots around the ship was the word SERVICE. It would require nothing less than service with an excellent spirit to please that large vacationing crowd and keep them coming back for more. It wasn't enough that the ship had cost eighteen billion dollars to build and was very beautiful and comfortable. Without an excellent spirit of service, the cruises could not have been successful.

> *To serve means to carry the same Spirit that was in Jesus when He came to this earth!*

An older couple sat with us at our table every evening. The man told me he had taken a cruise on another ship and had been very unhappy with the service. "I didn't leave a tip for any of them," he said. That other ship had also been an expensive one, with good food and a large staff, but the service had not been satisfactory.

Talent, money, good facilities, a wonderful organization ... it's all worthless unless the service is what it should be. You can have the best food around, but if it's not served well, you will surely lose your customers. Service is everything these days.

When we look at the attributes of Rebekah we can clearly see why God appointed her to become the bride of Isaac. Her greatest qualification was service. If you can serve, you can excel.

Never allow work to bring a prideful spirit to your heart. Remain humble and serve with an excellent spirit. That's what being a true Christian is all about.

ACCEPTING "HUMILIATING" JOBS

Let me open my heart and be very honest with you for a moment. I came to the U.S. from South Africa, where blacks made up a great majority of the forty-six million population. We whites were a minority of only about ten percent of the population, and we lived an above-average lifestyle. It was not unusual for us to have, at the very least, a full-time black housekeeper and a full-time black yardman. We considered this to be the way we helped the poor put food on their tables.

After I came here and saw how average Americans live, I had to admit that I had a lot of pride when it came to the performance of manual labor. I had rarely done it in my life, and somehow I considered it to be beneath my dignity. One of the first lessons I learned here was the dignity of work and the fact that no labor is dishonoring. I saw Americans doing tasks that only the poor performed in South Africa, tasks that I had long considered to be humiliating. Here, I also learned to do such things and know that doing them was not degrading in any way. Thank you, America, for teaching me that a true servant could care less about what particular work he is assigned.

SERVICE SHOWS RESPECT

Every true servant does his assigned work, not as an obligation, but as a service for someone he loves and respects. Too often, service is only rendered when there is respect for the person to be served, but Rebekah served someone she could not have respected—simply because she didn't yet know Abraham. She respected Eleazar as a human being, a visitor to her town and someone who needed water.

Rebekah served, without knowing Eleazar's master, because there was a need that someone had to meet. The heart of a true servant carries within it an automatic respect. Service without respect is never a genuine act of service. Instead, it comes across as arrogance.

THE TEST OF SERVICE

God tested Rebekah, and her test was to see how she would serve. The test was made more difficult because she was required to serve in an area in which she did not normally serve. If she had served Eleazar only (something that was clearly within her ability and would not have stretched her talents), she would have missed it. The test was to serve the ten camels, for what she did had to be something she could not or would not normally do.

> *What makes true servants so unique is that they serve in places and areas where pride would never enter!*

What makes true servants so unique is that they serve in places and areas where pride would never enter. Pride can serve, as long as the service suits it. True servants serve, whatever the appearance of things. Prideful people are very particular about whom they serve, but real servants serve, no matter who and what is involved. Rebekah was so genuine in her heart that serving the ten camels didn't bother her in the least.

True servants serve with ease. To them, it is never an

effort. Serving is what they do. A servant serves, not even knowing that he is doing anything extraordinary. He sees it as his duty, and, for him, it is the most satisfying thing he could possibly do in life. Prideful people, on the other hand, find serving in this way to be humiliating.

Although serving the camels was the test, it was an easy one for Rebekah. When serving is a thing of the heart, it is a blessing in itself to the person who performs the service. To the prideful, serving can be intensely painful.

One thing is clear: God never appoints unless He first tests. He loves everybody, but when it comes to promotion in His Kingdom, He requires that each of us be tested. And each test must be successfully passed before promotion is possible.

SERVING WITHOUT BEING ASKED

Another powerful sign of a true servant is that they do not have to be asked. Rebekah wasn't asked to serve Eleazar's camels. He asked her for a little water for himself, and she gladly gave it. But then she went the extra mile and offered to water the camels as well. Many serve, but only when they're specifically asked. True servants have the ability to see opportunities to serve where others see nothing. It could be said that a true servant serves the job before the job has been assigned to them.

Many people are heard to say, "I cannot do this [or that] because it's not my job." In a true servant's heart, there is never a question of who a job belongs to. They see it as a need that must be filled, and they set about to fill it.

Being Tested without Knowing That You're Being Tested

Most of us can pass any test if we have enough time to prepare for it. But being tested, without knowing that you're being tested or what the stakes are, is another matter entirely. True servants are ready for every test.

Rebekah was tested without knowing that she was being tested, and Abraham was also tested by God in this way. When God spoke to him to sacrifice Isaac, Abraham thought it was the "real deal." God revealed to him that it had been a test only after seeing that Abraham was willing to do whatever He asked of him.

Anyone can serve with excellence if they know it's not for real. Anyone can serve well when they know there's a good reward involved. A true servant serves—even if there is no reward at all.

If Abraham had known that he was being tested and what the reward would be, it would have been the easiest thing he had ever done. He didn't know, and you don't know either. So serve well. You never know who might be watching.

Service Is a Reward unto Itself

The eyes of a true servant are never upon the reward, but upon obedience to the master. Serving the master is a reward in itself.

A true servant can also never be discouraged. Discouragement comes when things don't work out as we expect them to, or the dividends are not as good as we might have imagined. For a servant, dividends don't enter into the equation. Rewards are the focus of a proud person. Who the master is ... that's what it's all about, for a true servant.

For Abraham to sacrifice his son *was* his reward. The reward was found in the honor to be obedient. And, to Abraham, this obedience was not a sacrifice; it was a privilege. Abraham never served God for the reward, for he didn't even know there would *be* a reward. We must not serve God for what we can receive, but for who He is. The most important thing for any true servant is not the reward, but knowing the master.

By the act of serving the camels, Rebekah revealed the true spirit of her heart, and through this, she stood out from the crowd. It is not the champion, pumped up with adrenaline, who catches the eye of God or the Mr. Know-It-All who stands out in His Kingdom. When God is the one making the choice, it is the spirit of the servant that catches His eye every time.

Jesus Is Our Example

Another servant in the Bible made the greatest impression ever made upon God, the Father. This Servant was none other than the King of kings and Lord of lords, the Resurrection and the Life Himself, Jesus Christ. He made His greatest impression under the cloak of a servant, and He became our example when it comes to servanthood.

In 2004, what I consider to be the greatest movie of all times was made: Mel Gibson's *Passion of the Christ*. I'm sure that those who love our Lord and understand eternal life will agree with this assessment. There were many outstanding things about the film, but the thing that made it so great, to my way of thinking, was its depiction of true servanthood. Jesus came to serve, and the highlight of His service was to give His life for us.

Can you imagine the hatred that must have existed in the people of Jesus' day for them to crucify a humble servant? It would have been completely understandable had they wanted to crucify someone who was arrogant or hateful, but how could they crucify a servant? Now, two thousand years later, the life of that Servant has changed the world. All the books in the world cannot contain what could be written about Him, and countless songs are sung about His exploits. His crucifixion forever split the world into two time periods: Before Christ and After Christ. Every servant makes a mark on his or her world.

REAL HUMILITY IN SERVICE

Many people serve because they seem to have no option, but that's nothing more than pride forced into submission. Real humility will be found where people have an option to walk away, but they choose to stay and serve anyway.

This is a prophetic picture of the end-time Church.

We will have beauty because of what Christ has done for us, and we will have reason, because of our attractiveness to Him, to be prideful. But the beauty of the end-time Church is that she will have the glory of the Lord upon her and still choose to serve in humility.

It was this spirit of a servant that was found in the life of Rebekah that became the major key to the capturing of her destiny. We all have a purpose and destiny in life, but having the wrong attitude toward life's issues can be disastrous. You can have all the giftings in the world, but if you have the wrong attitude toward those giftings, it can destroy you.

Anyone who wants to be great must learn to serve. To serve is to choose to become of less importance yourself and to allow the object you serve to become your master.

> *It would have been completely understandable had they wanted to crucify someone who was arrogant or hateful, but how could they crucify a servant?*

129

No one needs to tell a servant who the master is, and the master never needs to announce himself. The spirit of servanthood in a person enables them to quickly find the master. A servant cannot be humbled, because servanthood is humility itself, and humility is the nature of the true servant. True leaders will always serve, even when others are available to serve them.

To be a servant has nothing to do with humiliation or false humility. But service with true humility always leads to promotion.

SERVICE BRINGS PROMOTION

The day you become a servant, that's the first sign that greatness is coming your way. Being a servant will always bring you to a point where God can promote you. Godly promotion is destiny fulfilled, but prideful promotion is disaster. Among the women at the well at which Eleazar stopped, one found herself mightily blessed and destined for the best, and it was because she automatically began serving those hated animals that could have been easily ignored. Nothing is too small to serve when you have the heart of a servant. I firmly believe that if you could take every man and woman of greatness in God's Kingdom today and turn back the clock twenty or thirty years, you would find them all serving the camels of life.

SERVICE MAKES THE GIFT LOOK GOOD

The pitcher in Rebekah's hand was a tool used to

draw water, and that tool was only effective when it had been activated. Gifts are of no use at all unless they are activated and used to serve. Inactive tools become ornaments that eventually get in the way.

Even when a gift seems small, it can be used greatly. Surely Rebekah never imagined, when she left home with her pitcher, that she would be called upon to water ten camels. Like most of us, she probably had her own ideas about what her gift could and could not do. Until that day, her pitcher had been used only to draw water for her and her family. But now her gift would be used to serve in a much greater capacity.

I'm sure that we would all like to know just what that pitcher looked like. Gifts, to us, are very important. But, in reality, it was not the gift that was important in this situation. Because she had the spirit of a servant in her, Rebekah would have found a way to water the camels— even if she hadn't had that pitcher. It was not her gift that made her look good. It was her servant's spirit that made the gift look good. She was not chosen for the gifts she possessed. Rather, the spirit of a servant in her was the key to her successes and the only reason she was chosen.

If we could visit a museum today and look at or even touch the pitcher Rebekah used that day, many would do it, and they would ooh and aah when they saw it. But that pitcher was just her gift. What made it look great was the spirit behind it.

Most of us have a very low opinion of what we can accomplish in life, and that's because we compare our

> *When the right attitude is found in your heart, you will find that the gifts you have can go much further and accomplish much more that you might imagine!*

gifts with the needs before us. Never compare your pitcher with the many camels it will be called upon to serve. If you do, the task will usually appear impossible. But when you carry the right spirit, when the right attitude is found in your heart, you will find that the gifts you have can go much further and accomplish much more than you might imagine. The key is not the specific capacity of the particular pitcher you happen to have in your hand, but the spirit behind it. People who have very little in their hands, but who have the spirit of a servant, will accomplish much more than those who have great talents, but a wrong spirit.

MOTHER TERESA, A TRUE SERVANT

What was it that made a seemingly insignificant woman of India named Mother Teresa look so great? She never dressed in the latest designer fashions from Paris. She never participated in any modeling competition. If you looked at her appearance, you might have thought that she was herself a person in need. But in her heart she carried the spirit of a servant, and today the world recognizes her for the great servant she was.

Each year, awards are given to those who stand out because of their giftings in stage, screen, instrumental and vocal music, etc. Mother Teresa could never have competed in this arena, and yet she had something better. She had the heart of a servant.

ONE MAN'S ROAD TO SUCCESS

In the years before I came to the United States, I traveled extensively in ministry throughout South Africa. It was a lonely ministry that required going long distances. Every now and then, God gave me some younger man to travel with me, but, for the most part, I went alone.

At one point, one young man stayed with me for a longer-than-usual period, and I tried to help him find the mind of Christ for his own future. To most people, he seemed oddly out of place, somehow unfit for the job. For some reason, he had never been motivated or inspired by his peers to reach out for his destiny. It seemed that he rarely gave a thought to his future, and, worse, he did things that caused others to be wary of him.

At times, I wondered if I was wrong to encourage him. He did have his faults, after all, and maybe I should just let him go his way. Then, God began to plant a seed of thought in me, something that I believe to this day. He loves the underdog, and I knew from that moment on that God wanted to help this young man and to raise him up.

One certain week, I was booked to minister Sunday through Wednesday in a church several hundred miles away from the city where I lived, and I supposed I would have to take public transportation again. Then, this young man, whom many had rejected, came to me and said he would be willing to take me to that town early on Sunday morning. He would have to leave me there and return home that night in order to work Monday through Wednesday. But after work on Wednesday, he would again drive those hundreds of miles to be with me in my last meeting. Then, after the meeting, he would take me home. He was willing to do all that, just so I would not have to travel alone or be inconvenienced. Needless to say, I was absolutely overwhelmed by this unusual act of kindness. How could I ever forget such an act of service? This young man helped me when I needed it most.

In the early morning hours, as we were traveling back to our town together, I was startled to hear him say, "When you prophesied to the people tonight, I knew every time what you were about to tell them." I thought about this for a moment before answering him: "Then this is the mantel of anointing that is coming over you." He believed it, and it happened. Today this young man is traveling across America in ministry. Many go to his meetings, trying to tap into the anointing he has. How remarkable! He never attended Bible school a day in his life. So, how can we explain such a phenomenon?

I think I have the answer. Because this young man was willing to serve where no one else would, God rewarded him in an extraordinary way. Now, many would pay anything to receive the same reward. Those who can carry the mantel of servanthood are destined for great honor and promotion.

This particular man had some things in his life that were wrong, and so men overlooked him and didn't consider him to be a candidate for God's blessing. But God didn't overlook him. I can only imagine today how difficult it must be for many of those who rejected him to admit how wrong they were and to acknowledge the mantel the man carries. God is not a man, He doesn't think like we do, and He promotes those whom He chooses. This man's pitcher was not very attractive, but he was willing to take a man of God from point A to point B. It's people like that whom God keeps in mind for promotion. And He delights in lifting up the underdogs of life.

Your Gift Must Serve to Quench Thirst

Rebekah watered ten camels, filling twenty stomachs, using a small pitcher, and she didn't stop until they were all satisfied. The spirit of a servant serves until the end, and the end comes only when everyone is satisfied. Serve until everyone is satisfied, until everyone has had enough. Serve until every need is met.

That seemingly insignificant pitcher was the gift that

saved men and animals from dying of thirst. It's great to serve people of money or position, but true servants serve the need. Rebekah served those who were thirsty, those who were desperate, and she became, for them, the difference between life and death. You can live without money, but you can't live without water. She served the need of a man and his beasts of burden, but Jesus served the needs of the whole world. He readily supplies our thirst for salvation, healing and deliverance. He was God's gift to the world, but He was much more than that. He became our servant, and He bore our sins, creating a way for us to enter Heaven. He delighted in serving the needs of all mankind. Let us strive to be more like Him.

In the right circumstance, any man would give all that he has for water. And if water is the thing that's needed, no pitcher used to bring it would ever be considered insignificant. So often, when we have plenty of water available to us, we're picky about the water we drink and the vessel we drink it from. But truly thirsty people are never concerned about what the container that carries the water may look like.

EGOTISTICAL SERVICE SPELLS DISASTER

Many gifts are impressive, but they can't seem to carry any water. Pitchers carry water, and you and I need one, for we are called to serve the world around us with something that is lifesaving. We are called to rescue the perishing. Still, after being in ministry for many years, many of us fall into the dreadful habit of serving up something that fails to quench people's thirst. What a tragedy!

We must do an efficiency check on ourselves from time to time by asking simple questions. Am I still relevant in what I do? Do I still serve the purpose of Christ? Does my life promote Jesus? Or has it become too much about myself?

When your ministry has become about yourself, it becomes very important to you that your pitcher shine. Many spend great amounts of time polishing their gift and making it look more professional, but while they're doing that, are they serving anyone?

I will be the first to say that we must stay relevant, stay on the cutting edge of things and not fall behind. But we cannot afford to spend months and years working on our image. What good is image if you're unproductive? There comes a time when you must be satisfied with who you are and what you have and then

> *Rebekah served those who were thirsty, those who were desperate, and she became, for them, the difference between life and death!*

start focusing on the thirst of others (not on how professional you look as you're serving them).

If you cannot serve water to the thirsty when no one's watching you and when the cameras are not focused on you, then you have no right to serve them when the camera's are turned on. When that is the case, your intention is not pure. Serve where you are with what you now have, and later you can think about upgrading your pitcher.

David served the sheep on the hillside where no one could see him, and the sheep could not reward him. Sheep are not very intelligent creatures and may not even know you have served them. Never be concerned about who will reward you. If that is your concern, your priorities are still wrong.

Eleazar now knew that he had found the woman he sought because Rebekah willingly served his smelly and noisy camels—without even being asked to do it. That's the spirit of Christ, and its presence always leads to promotion in the Kingdom of God.

CHAPTER 9

THE YOUNG WOMAN
WAS VERY BEAUTIFUL

Now the young woman was very beautiful to behold,
a virgin; no man had known her.   Genesis 24:16

Something needs to be said about the beauty of
Rebekah, but it must not be overemphasized. Clearly the
Scriptures do not attempt to hide the fact that she was
beautiful. This young woman had an outer beauty that
could captivate men, and many might immediately take
for granted that this was to be her ticket to success. That
was not the case.

As a very attractive and industrious woman, of course,
Rebekah could have used her natural beauty and talent
to accomplish her goals in life and to gain favor with
others. She chose not to do this. Her beauty is mentioned
in the Scriptures, not as a major consideration of her
worthiness to become the bride of Isaac, but only in passing. She was beautiful, but that was not what made her
great.

CHOOSING YOUR METHOD

This is an important point. There are many ways to accomplish our goals in life. We each have natural talents that can help us on our way to desired accomplishments. And Rebekah's natural beauty could have been used. Instead, she chose to use another giftedness that was in her life, and that worked for her. Rebekah's destiny was to marry Isaac, but it was not her outward beauty that qualified her for that privilege; it was her willingness to serve.

Rebekah's outer beauty is typical of the Church. The Church is definitely covered in a beauty that attracts God, and yet He desires much more of her. The ultimate beauty, the one that would impress Eleazar, the type of the Holy Spirit, was the servant's heart Rebekah revealed. This was her greatest beauty and the thing that would qualify her for promotion.

> *Rebekah's destiny was to marry Isaac, but it was not her outward beauty that qualified her for that privilege; it was her willingness to serve!*

OUTER BEAUTY FADES

Outer beauty is sometimes age restrictive, but inner beauty is everlasting, and the thing in you that God is after is the everlasting beauty. Outer beauty is seasonal, but inner beauty is not restricted by mere looks. As the years pass and the natural beauty of youth begins to fade, you can still qualify as beautiful with God—if your true qualification comes from within. Outer beauty can be taken away, but inner beauty will be with you until the day you die.

The beauty of Rebekah was great enough to be mentioned, and that was not true of every woman of the Bible. So, it had a certain significance. Hers was not a beauty that could only be appreciated by the man who would love her and make her his own. Rather, everyone recognized her beauty. But it was not her beauty that convinced Eleazar that she was the woman he sought. When she served, without knowing what was about to happen or whom she was really serving, then he was convinced. That was her real beauty in God's sight. She played her role well, for this is what the Church of today and the future Bride of Christ should be like.

Many women used this particular well of water, and there must have been many beautiful ones among them. In order to catch Eleazar's eye, however, the chosen one would have to stand out among all the rest. And the one major characteristic that stood out in the life of Rebekah was the fact that she had the true spirit of a servant. This was the one thing that allowed her to catch Eleazar's eye.

If you have the right spirit, you will do the right thing at the right time and still not know you did something important, and such a beauty is more than skin deep.

It is possible to have many giftings in life and still miss the mark. Rebekah, although she was physically attractive, could have missed her date with Isaac. In the end, she had what it took, and that was not a special hairdo or the ability to wear new styles well. She went much deeper than that.

As we have seen, pride is the enemy of service, and beauty is, all too often, a motivation for pride. When a woman is attractive and knows she is attractive, it's a danger to her soul. Of natural beauty, the Scriptures say:

Charm is deceitful and beauty is passing,
But a woman who fears the LORD, she shall be praised.
                                                        Proverbs 31:30

Surely, Rebekah had been told that she was beautiful, probably many times, but that fact had not spoiled her spirit.

HER BEAUTY AND HER PITCHER

Rebekah had two major gifts that were evident at the well that day. One was her outer beauty, and the other was the pitcher she had in her hand. Both of these gifts could be seen with the natural eye, both gifts came from God's hand, but neither of them would become the key to her life, the thing that would take her to greatness. Of the two, however, the pitcher was the most significant.

To Rebekah, her beauty without a pitcher was worthless. The simplicity of the thing in her hand was the thing God would use. Knowing how people think, we can imagine that her natural beauty probably drew more people to her than the pitcher did, but God was not impressed by it. He knew where her real talents rested.

There is way too much professional beauty in the Church today and not nearly enough true servanthood. The result is that many are still dying of thirst. Whatever can serve water is the key gift today, and it needs to be used with the spirit of a true servant.

Having things will also not necessarily help you meet the needs of others. Things are of no value unless they are put to use. The things you possess must be controlled and administrated by a spirit of service.

Many people have "things," and having those "things" only makes them arrogant. It would be better for prideful people not to have a gift at all. Many people have the ability to impress us with their outward beauty and talents, but when they open their mouths, there is no substance to them. The beauty was important and the pitcher was important, but even more important was the spirit of the servant behind them.

Rebekah must surely have been tempted to use her beauty to impress Eleazar, but if she had done that, he would have seen very quickly that she did not possess the spirit he sought. A true servant is always beautiful because he or she serves to rescue others from disaster and death. That was the ministry of Jesus, and He was beautiful.

OUTER BEAUTY ONLY GOES SO FAR

Beauty, talent and personal aspirations can buy you a certain level of success, but true servanthood can shape you and move you to positions of authority and power that no man can offer. Even though Rebekah could have used her beauty to impress Eleazar, she chose to serve him instead.

The Spirit-Filled Life Bible says of Rebekah: "Rebekah's name refers to 'tying or binding,' implying that her beauty was so great, it could literally 'captivate' or 'fascinate' men." If you have the power to fascinate or captivate, why would you need to serve? Rebekah clearly had the tools necessary to be fascinating and captivating in her own right, and she could have easily controlled and manipulated others with her beauty. Instead, she chose the humility of service. I have seen many people in ministry using certain giftings to fascinate or captivate, and this can be a very dangerous practice. When you know you have gifts in certain areas of your life, be careful how you use them. Make sure they glorify God.

If you can fascinate or captivate, why serve? If you can win a man over with your natural gifts, why not? As we have seen, the problem is that natural beauty is seasonal. When you lose your outer beauty, then what will you use to impress the people around you? Rebekah won the heart of Eleazar with something she would have long after losing her natural beauty. She won his favor with her servant's spirit.

Natural beauty might serve us well ... just as long as that beauty lasts, but having the spirit of a servant will serve us well into eternity. Even when she was old, Rebekah would still have the benefits that living life with the spirit of a servant brought. Make sure you know where your motivation is coming from.

On the cross, men destroyed the beauty of Jesus' physical body, but they couldn't destroy the spirit of the servant in Him. This spirit can never be destroyed. The body might be destroyed, but the spirit lives on.

> *Natural beauty might serve us well ... just as long as that beauty lasts!*

Nothing Quite Like It!

Oh, beloved, I desire to be filled with this anointing for service, for there is nothing quite like it. Let us serve, for this is the greatest thing we could ever hope to accomplish in life.

A ministry can never be built on captivating and manipulating. Any gift that is fleshly is restricted to time; it is seasonal, but the spirit of being a servant was something that would stay with Rebekah for a lifetime. What you are in the spirit now is what you will be in eternity.

Allow the Holy Spirit to make you into the being that you need to be in order to serve well in the moment of unknowingly serving your destiny. Before you can walk into your destiny, you need to serve toward it. People don't seem to realize that what they do today directly influences their future in the most dramatic terms.

As we have learned, when Rebekah served Eleazar, she was actually serving her own destiny. Her physical beauty would have done nothing to bring that about. And the thing that will take you to your destiny is possessing the spirit of a servant. Learn this lesson today, and you will prosper in God's Kingdom tomorrow.

CHAPTER 10

SHE HASTENED AND LET HER PITCHER DOWN

Then she hastened and let her pitcher down to her hand, and gave him a drink.   Genesis 24:18

As Christians, we must make sure that when we present Christ from our pulpits and through our testimonies we always present His Word in such a way that it does not become a dry presentation that frustrates people and fails to quench their thirst. Anything we do that does not satisfy thirst is done in vain. Thirst that is not satisfied destroys the soul.

Mere busyness can often be deceiving and make us feel that we're somehow doing the right thing. The important question is this: Are our lives supplying water that quenches the thirst of others? Are we making any significant difference to their needs?

WILLINGNESS AND READINESS

The Spirit-Filled Life Bible further says of Rebekah: "[Rebekah] is introduced as a diligently industrious and beautifully sensitive girl. Her willingness to serve Eleazar and her readiness to draw water for all ten of the thirsty camels dramatizes this." The two key words here are *willingness* and *readiness.* We are not always ready, even if we are willing.

The readiness referred to here was all about drawing water for the ten camels. In simple language, it meant a lot of hard work. There are certain things that we're willing to do, but we're not ready to do, and there are other things that we're ready to do, but we're not willing to do. Willingness and readiness must meet if we are to accomplish great things.

Rebekah was willing to serve Eleazar, so that was easier, but serving the camels was another story entirely. With the camels, however, even though she might not have been very willing (meaning that she was not exactly looking forward to the task at hand), she made herself ready for it.

Readiness does not always imply a complete willingness. Readiness often requires that we go beyond what is comfortable for us. We go beyond feelings, and we go beyond experience. Readiness takes over where complete willingness may be lacking, and this is when true servanthood is revealed.

I can make myself ready to do things in life that I don't particularly enjoy, but I'm always more willing to do things I like. Rebekah looked at the camels and realized that watering them was a tall order. Still, she immediately included the camels in her offer. She was both willing and ready, a winning combination.

We must go further than just being willing. Let us do the things that we're unwilling to do, and, in this way, go beyond the call of duty. This is the spirit of Christ.

Camels usually fall outside the category of willingness, and many can only serve inside that circle. God expects us to serve outside of our comfort zone, serving even in the unexpected. What is "the unexpected"? Those are the camels of unknown ownership and purpose that will show up in your life from time to time.

> *Readiness does not always imply a complete willingness!*

Like many others today, you may not be ready to do the things that go beyond your present willingness. A servant, however, will serve—even when the going is tough. Jesus definitely felt pain on that cross. It was, in no way, a pleasant experience, something that He looked forward to. Still, He went there because He was both ready and willing. Let readiness and willingness come together.

These days, we love to specify in advance what our job description will be. When we take on a new job, the first thing that needs to be discussed and defined is the job description. Employers are eager to ask new applicants to sign a contract that will explain their exact job description. Why? In this modern day, we are more pay-oriented than we are service-oriented. We want to know what the minimum is that we need to do in order to earn a certain amount of money. With true servants, job descriptions are not needed, for servants will always go beyond what is required of them. They do the things that others are neither ready nor willingly to do.

The absence of true servants has brought our society to a place where a contract is necessary to secure a certain standard of service. What happened to the days when someone's word was worth as much or more than their signature on a piece of paper?

Workers are promoted on the basis of their labor, but servants are appointed to the highest offices. A contract binds a worker to do certain things, but a servant would only find such a contract limiting, since he always does much more than is required of him.

THE PAIN OF SERVING

Serving is not without pain. In serving the camels, Rebekah, being a woman, must have experienced some discomfort. Jesus' entire life and His death on the cross were all about serving, and it was a painful process. Serving will strip you of your strength.

Jesus served until He had no more strength left. He served until He felt weak. Still, as He hung there on the cross, He was both willing and ready. The end-time Church will be made up of those who are willing and ready to go the extra mile. God is carefully watching those who fall into this category, and He will promote them to stand next to His Son, for they have taken on His likeness.

Prideful people go up before they go down, but humble people go down before they go up. The same God who humiliates prideful people is the God who promotes humble people. Prideful people live without the pain of sacrifice, but they end up in the pain of humiliation. A servant starts out with the pain of humiliation, but ends up in pain-free exaltation. Although being a servant looks like humiliation, it is not. It may be humiliating in the eyes of the prideful, but in the eyes of God, it is the highest level of service.

THE FRAGRANCE OF A SERVANT

Hand-in-hand with being a servant goes a fragrance. Pride has a smell to it, and so does humility. Humility does not need any announcement. It announces itself. Somebody who is humble does not even know it. It's amazing that even prideful people don't know that they're prideful. In Rebekah's life, the fragrance, or aroma, of her servant's heart ultimately became so strong that it overshadowed her outer beauty.

When Jesus died, everyone (even His enemies) knew that a servant had just passed from this life. There was a fragrance that hung in the air just after His crucifixion, and it influenced the whole world. To this day, that fragrance still hangs over the earth, and it will be with us until the end of time.

I believe that most people, by now, have seen Mel

Gibson's movie *"The Passion of the Christ."* When I left the movie theater after watching this movie, I was overwhelmed with something that (even until this day) I cannot explain. The fragrance that came out of the heart of that Servant hung over me, and I find it difficult to put into words. The only words that came to me as I saw it are inadequate. Dying on that cross was one thing, but the fragrance it left behind is simply indescribable.

> *Jesus was a servant, and if and when He truly comes into your life, then you will become a servant too!*

Why did a movie star from Hollywood choose to produce such a movie about the crucifixion? This is the story of the cross, a story that many have thought was a "boring" one. Still, the attendance at his movie was record-breaking. Wasn't it just a movie about a man who died on a cross? No, a thousand times no. It was much more than that.

One of the keys to the impact of this film (and there are many) was the fact that Jesus served the human race, and the fragrance of love that came out of His sacrifice influences the world to this day and will influence the world for all eternity. Such a fragrance can only come forth from being a true servant.

A true servant will ultimately become the one being served. So, if you want to be served, then serve. Because Christ served, today there are many millions who are willing to serve Him, and we will serve Him throughout all eternity.

THE SPIRIT OF SERVICE

You cannot *learn* how to serve. Serving others is a spirit, the spirit of Jesus Christ. He was a servant, and if and when He truly comes into your life, then you will become a servant too. If you are a believer in Christ and you're not a servant, it shows that you have lost something He originally placed in you when you were born again. When you gave Him your life and allowed Him to take over and live His life through you, you had to become a servant. What happened to that spirit?

It is impossible to serve Christ and be prideful because He's not prideful, and serving Christ means that He lives in you. If you're no longer a servant, that's a confirmation that you're not on the trail He originally placed you on. No one can live at His feet and continue to walk in pride. The presence of pride in your life is an indication that you have turned away from Him, at least to some degree, for He is the complete manifestation of what a servant should be.

GOD SEVERELY TESTED ABRAHAM

True servants will be tested, just as Rebekah was tested

before she could be appointed as the appropriate bride for Isaac.

We are all impressed with what we read about Abraham. God went out of His way to bless this man, and this blessing was directly connected to the testing of Abraham's character. We looked at it, in part, in Chapter 1, but let's take another look now:

> *By Myself I have sworn, says the Lord, because you have done this thing, and have not withheld your son, your only son, in blessing I will bless you, and in multiplying I will multiply your descendents as the stars of the heaven and as the sand which is on the seashore; and your descendants shall possess the gate of their enemies.* Genesis 22:16-17

These are strong words, words that God does not use everyday. He said that He would bless Abraham because he had *"done this thing."* What was the *"thing"* that Abraham had done that impressed God to use such strong language? It was an act of obedience.

There is nothing that impresses God more than obedience. Obedience is the covenant partner of humility. To be obedient is to serve. Prideful people tend not to be very obedient. Their obedience is to themselves. Obedience to yourself does not mean that you are necessarily obedient to God.

Earlier, the Scriptures had stated:

God tested Abraham.   Genesis 22:1

The unique thing about this case was that Abraham, as we have seen, didn't know that what he was experiencing was a test. If he had known about the test, he could have prepared for it. But most of God's tests are given in this way—without previous warning.

God asked Abraham the most difficult thing you can ever ask of anyone: to sacrifice his own flesh and blood, the son he loved so dearly, Isaac. God knew very well how much Abraham loved this son, and that's why sacrificing Isaac became the test.

God doesn't ask us for things we merely "like." There's a great difference between what I *like* and what I *love,* and godly promotion will always require a sacrifice of your own flesh, something you love more than anything else. Things we *like* can sometimes be given away, but things we *love* must be torn from us. This is what sacrifice is all about. Giving up things we simply *like* is usually not a sacrifice because they can be replaced.

God's intention in all of this was never to sacrifice Isaac. God is and always has been against human sacrifice. He just wanted to see how far Abraham would trust Him.

Abraham Passed the Test

Abraham didn't waste time in responding to God, and he also took pains to be sure that he would not be tempted to compromise. He separated from the other young men of his company, lest he be tempted to substitute one of them for Isaac.

It also impressed God that Abraham called the place where he had been sent to sacrifice his son the place where the two of them would go and *"worship"* (Genesis 22:5). It was to be the place of his greatest pain and suffering, and yet because he was doing it for God, to Abraham, it was *"worship."* That surely touched the Father's heart.

What do you call your place of greatest pain? How many times we murmur when we go through difficult times! And yet Abraham called the place where He would pay the greatest price to prove his loyalty to God his place of *"worship."* That tells us everything about the incredible relationship Abraham had with God. No wonder God was impressed with him!

When we look at the wonderful reward Abraham received, it gives us a better understanding of how very much God honors obedience. Your act of obedience to God will cause Him to go to the uttermost to bless you. Obedience is the one thing that will trigger God to swear by Himself and bring a blessing upon you and me that will surpass our wildest dreams.

Every unexpected test that you pass will bring the blessings of a lifetime upon you. Sacrifice comes before greatness, and it gives birth to greatness. The sacrifice of Christ on the cross made Him the Champion of all ages.

Abraham, because he was obedient and passed the test, didn't have to sacrifice Isaac. The thing you think you will lose will never be lost—unless you are disobedient to God. Obedience will not only bring to you the utmost blessing of God, but it will also secure what you love.

Like Rebekah, Abraham served, and both of them were promoted to a level of blessing the human mind cannot quite comprehend. Obedience and service go hand in hand. Those who do not believe in this need to re-read the Bible. Service is the only way to promotion.

SERVICE IS TO OTHERS

There were many women at this particular well, but not all of them served with the same intensity as Rebekah. Many only served themselves. Serving your own needs does not make you a servant. If you only feed yourself, you don't qualify. Service, by definition, is always to others.

How many times we murmur when we go through difficult times!

When you have a servant's spirit, you always consider the needs of others first, and you serve them before you serve yourself. To serve means to forget about your own needs and to focus, instead, on the needs of others.

Many years ago, I attended an event where a certain pastor, who was greatly blessed by God with a powerful singing voice, would be the featured artist. The man was taking the church world by storm. In no time at all, his products were being sold all over South Africa, and his name is a household name there even to this day. I was soon to discover the reason.

That night, the venue where he would sing would be packed to capacity. I was very fortunate to have a seat in the first row and was honored to be afforded such a prominent seat.

After all the available seating had been filled, people continued to come, and so extra chairs had to be quickly set out to accommodate them. Still, they kept coming, until the ushers had a hard time keeping up with them. It was an unbelievably large crowd by South African standards.

Suddenly, I saw something I never anticipated. The pastor, the artist who had came from afar to sing and would be the main attraction that night, got up from his place and began helping the ushers carry in more chairs. He grabbed others and appointed them to see that everyone got seated.

This act took many by surprise. Here was a man who had achieved national attention, and yet he was not above helping to seat the people that night. Many others, who were known only in some local setting, would never have done it.

I was never more impressed. I knew that I was watching a real servant of God, and yet I was equally sure that he wasn't aware of the great thing he was doing. He was serving ordinary people, and according to the culture of the time, he should not have been handling chairs. But true servants are ready and willing to wait on the nobodies of this world, and they don't wait to be asked.

There's a reason this man's singing ministry reached a level of national honor. Personally, I believe that what made him so unique was the beauty of his servant spirit, combined with his singing talent. I was impressed with his singing talent that night, but I also saw a beauty in him that surpassed the talent. He had the spirit of a true servant.

Before he could win the hearts of the crowd that night by singing to them, he had already won them by serving them and revealing his servant spirit. There is no work too dirty or too unimportant for a servant. Servants never classify work. Work, to them, is something that needs to be done to satisfy a need, and that is their purpose in life.

A WELL WITHOUT A SERVANT

What good is a church without the spirit of a servant or a ministry without the heart of a servant? The completion of the well wasn't the water. Water without a servant to serve it doesn't quench thirst. Church facilities cannot meet the needs of people. It is the servant at the well who completes the picture. Never lose your gifting, and never lose the spirit of excellence in which you do things, but remember, above all else, we need the spirit of a servant.

Jesus was the Son of God. He was at the right hand of God the Father and was one of the members of the

Godhead. He was divine, had never known sin and had no personal reason whatsoever to come to this sinful world. Still, although He had all the attributes of being God, He was humble enough to come here and serve us.

Have we become too professional in the Church today? Being professional and doing things in a spirit of excellence should not destroy the spirit of servanthood in us. Instead, it is the spirit of a servant that drives us to want to do things in a spirit of excellence, to do them professionally. A servant who truly serves well will serve to the last detail. Rebekah proved that.

> *Have we become too professional in the Church today?*

GOING FURTHER

Rebekah not only served at the well. She went further when she later served Eleazar with lodging for the night. Then she served the camels again, this time with straw and feed. Her desire to serve was not just a onetime event. It was a continuing reality.

Losing the spirit of servanthood is to lose your credibility. To lose your servanthood is to lose your right to call yourself a servant of the Lord. Have you lost your heart to serve the community as a church? If so, you have lost your right to exist as a church. Serve as Jesus served, and you will be destined for a journey of promotion.

The amazing thing about Jesus was that He was Holiness Himself, and yet He was still willing to serve. He demonstrated the utmost act of obedience in the form of total humility. My personal conclusion is that true holiness creates true humility. A truly anointed man of God will always remain humble.

Today, when men become successful, the first thing that surfaces is pride, and that spells trouble. If you and I are as anointed as we think we are, why aren't we more willing to serve others?

Let's be clear. The true anointing knows no pride. Truly anointed people are approachable and easy to communicate with. This is the test of a true ministry. Jesus was always available for the people around Him, even when the disciples thought they should be sent away.

SERVING IN YOUR ASSIGNED PLACE

Rebekah must have drawn water from this well many times before. The well was not an unfamiliar site to her. She was one of the regulars there. The day she served Eleazar was just another day of drawing water. This time, her steadfastness and her faithfulness brought her a great reward. She did not find her destiny just because of being at the well, but destiny found her because of her obedience there.

And, remember, the well it a type of the local church. It is vitally important that we be faithful to the church where God has placed us. Being faithful at the place of her responsibility, Rebekah found destiny and purpose.

Many times we run after open doors and opportunities, as if we needed to help God. It is more important for God to find us faithful in the small things in life, rather than running after great things and, because of it, being absent from the well where He has placed us.

Serve with faithfulness at the well of your responsibilities, and He will send someone to come and find you right where you are. Remember, the water and the pitcher in your hand is a needed commodity, and, at the right time, someone will visit your well with a thirst that needs to be quenched. Being in your assigned place will bring to you the greatest fulfillment in your life.

Find your well, position yourself there for service, and let the promotion come as God sees fit. At the right time, He will show up. The Bridegroom desires a bride, and when the season comes for her to be identified, you must be in your place. This need for a bride must be met and will be met, and you can be the chosen one—if you are found in your place, positioned at the well to serve.

The local church, according to the Bible, is the place where the Lord must find us serving His purposes, and yet many, in these modern days, fail to recognize the importance of the local church. How sad that they will be somewhere else, running after greatness, when Eleazar comes in search of them.

The strength of a church is not in some mighty man of God coming in to bless it, but in the members of the church themselves. Find a church so that God can find you. Find a well, for He will visit you there. Then, stand beside it faithfully.

THE DIFFERENCE BETWEEN WELLS AND BROOKS

There are wells, and there are brooks, and the two are very different. A brook is a small stream of water that may, at some point, dry up. A well, however, is not fed by surface water, and therefore, it remains constant—even in times of drought.

Which is best? A well? Or a brook? A well is better, of course. The brook may be more visible and catch our attention, but a well is set deep within the earth where its waters are protected. Few people would drink from a brook, but millions of people worldwide depend on wells for the water they need.

What does this mean to you? Serve in a church where there is some depth of experience and teaching, and don't be guilty of running after the little brooks that may look good for a while, but rarely last. A brook can be a blessing, but in times of drought, you need a deep well.

God is drawn toward faithfulness, not the attractiveness of the well. Greatness is birthed out of faithfulness, and faithfulness will take you to your destiny. The hope of destiny in you should make you want to serve at the well where God has placed you, and this faithful service will be the thing that takes you to the ultimate purpose for your life.

CHAPTER 11

WONDERING AT HER

And the man, wondering at her, remained silent.

Genesis 24:21

This is one of my favorite verses. Rebekah stirred the heart of Eleazar, and she didn't even know she was doing it. He wondered at her, meaning he stared at her. He focused on her. His mind and thoughts were captivated by her. And, remember, Eleazar is a type of the Holy Spirit, and Rebekah is a type of the Church.

When we serve, God's Spirit is impressed with us. The spirit of servanthood in us impresses God so that He cannot keep His eye off of us. Rebekah brought Eleazar to a standstill, and you can do the same with the Spirit of the living God today.

God is watching us; He has His eyes on us. Oh, may He find us faithful in difficult times. May He find us faithful when we're not even aware that He's watching. Anyone can serve well (if they know they're being watched), but it takes a real servant to serve well when they don't realize that anyone is watching.

God's Eye Is Upon Us

Eleazar could not remove his eye from Rebekah. His eyes followed her wherever she moved. She was marked by him. Without her knowledge, she was just steps from becoming the bride of Isaac. She had already been promoted, and she didn't even know it. Only later would she hear what had happened and know the importance of the man she was even now serving.

> *Rebekah had already been promoted, and she didn't even know it!*

It would all take a little while to come to fruition, but the fact of the matter was that Rebekah, in that moment of service, actually became the bride of Isaac, son of perhaps the richest man upon the face of the earth. What an overwhelming thought! By serving well in your present capacity, you have already qualified yourself for a future appointment. Rebekah, by serving, had already connected with her destiny. She just didn't know it yet. And the same may be true of you.

God's eye is upon us. His mind is made up concerning you and me. His plan for your life is final. He saw you being faithful in difficult times, and He decided right then and there that you were doing so well that He couldn't help but bless you.

Can you imagine God watching you because you've

done something that impresses Him? What a wonderful thought!

GOD'S GIFTS ARE WAITING

It wouldn't be long before Eleazar began to give Rebekah gifts of gold and silver. Once you've caught the eye of God, no one will be able to keep your gold and silver from you.

In order for us to serve well, we need to be filled with the Spirit of the living God. Only the Spirit of God in us can make us the servants we need to be. To be filled with the Holy Spirit is to be filled with the Spirit of a servant. Jesus demonstrated that Spirit of a servant when He served even in His death. Pride can never die for anything, but the spirit of being a servant can overcome pride. Let us bow down before our Master, becoming what He wants to make of us.

Oh, that I may be found worthy when He puts His eyes on me. Oh, that I may do the thing that will stir His heart. I trust that this is your prayer as well.

SILENCE IS NOT ALWAYS BAD

The moment Rebekah served the camels, it so stirred the heart of Eleazar that he became speechless, and he remained silent for a time. Sometimes silence is a sign of overwhelming satisfaction. Sometimes words cannot describe the moment of great fulfillment. Rebekah had just performed the act that qualified her for marrying Abraham's son. That left Eleazar speechless.

Being led by the Spirit of God, we will do things that will stir the heart of God in such a way that silence will be the answer. I can imagine that, in that moment, Eleazar said in his heart: "This is the one. Mission complete! Task fulfilled! Thank You, Lord!"

My dear friend, God's eye is upon you. He is watching you. He is following you. Just by serving Him, you have done exactly what He was expecting of you. What more could we desire than to have the eye of God watching us? You have left Him speechless.

Please don't interpret the silence of God in your life as negative. That silence just might be a sign of His approval for what you have done. Many times, we interpret silence as a sign that God has forgotten about us. In this case, silence represents the time He needs to prepare Himself to tell you that you've just qualified for promotion. Praise God!

RACHAEL VS. LEAH

Many of the lessons of Genesis 24 can be seen again in the life of Rebekah's future son Jacob. Isaac and Rebekah eventually had two sons, twins, Esau and Jacob. At one point, Jacob went to live with his Uncle Laban. Laban asked Jacob what he wanted as payment for his labor, and Jacob answered that he wanted his daughter Rachel as his wife (Genesis 29:15-18). Rachel had an older sister, Leah, and this was to cause some serious family problems, and from it we can learn a lot.

Rachael: A Type of Our Dreams

Rachael was beautiful in form and appearance, and she represents our dreams. Our dreams are always attractive. We all have such dreams, and often they are what keep us running another race and working toward another prize. No part of our dreams is ever bad.

Jacob chose to serve seven years for his dream, and no sacrifice is ever too challenging when it comes to our dreams. Seven years seemed to him as just a few days because he was so in love with this woman.

Leah: A Type of Reality

If Rachel was beautiful, Leah was just the opposite. Jacob chose Rachael and declared his willingness to serve seven years for her. He never asked for Leah, and yet that's what he got. Reality never seems to be nearly as beautiful as our dreams.

It happened like this: When the seven years were up, Jacob asked for his wife. The word that he used was *wife*, and the fact that he used this word shows that he felt that he now possessed his dream. He deserved Rachel, for he had worked hard for her. Seeming to agree, Laban immediately began preparing a feast and inviting guests, and the wedding was on.

We all know well the story of what happened next. It was an evening wedding, and by the time the happy couple got to their bed, it was very dark. The next morning, when Jacob awoke and turned to look into the face of his beloved, he received the shock of his life. There was

Leah in his bed. Reality had just set in. This was not what Jacob had dreamed of, nor what he had asked for. Before the beauty of your dreams can be fulfilled, the reality of life must come to you.

Jacob immediately went to his father-in-law and demanded an accounting. Was it not for Rachael that he had agreed to labor? Why, then, had he been deceived in this way? In our seasons of questioning and misunderstandings, we need to know that God is in total control of our lives, and He knows just what to deliver to us and when.

Laban asked Jacob to serve another seven years for Rachael. This was asking a lot, seeing that Jacob had learned the hard way. His first seven years of service seemed to have been in vain. Amazingly, he agreed, and he went on to serve another seven years for the woman he loved. Dreams are more appreciated for what they really are once you have paid a greater price than you, at first, anticipated you might.

Leah Was Unloved

After seven years, Rachael no longer looked the way she had when Jacob had first seen her. Still, he loved her, and this led to him neglecting Leah. After being married to his dream, he found it very difficult to continue the relationship with Leah. She was not naturally attractive, and, on top of that, there seemed to be something wrong with her eyes. Again, she was a type of what life can be all about—the reality of day-to-day living.

Then a powerful thing happened to change all of their

lives. When all of this drama had finally reached a climax, God took things into His own hands and did something totally unexpected:

When the Lord saw that Leah was unloved, He opened her womb; but Rachael was barren.
Genesis 29:31

Before the beauty of your dreams can be fulfilled, the reality of life must come to you!

In the difficult seasons of our life, if you and I cannot be faithful to the things that seem to be negative and unattractive, God will not allow us to bear fruit with our dream. He had been watching Jacob all the time, and he wasn't happy with his attitude. When it had finally gone too far, He stepped in and taught Jacob the lesson of his life.

Because Leah was unattractive, she had not been his choice for a life mate. She had just shown up, unannounced and unwanted. She was not someone Jacob felt he could be proud of, and therefore, he was not about to have children by her. Because God knew what Jacob needed and gave him Leah, He expected Jacob to treat her differently. Jacob, however, closed his heart to her and favored

Rachael instead. It must have come as a great shock to him, then, that Leah would be the wife who gave him sons.

Having a son was the greatest honor a woman of that time could hope for. In bearing sons, a woman not only honored herself; she honored her husband and won his undying love. Rachel, Jacob's beloved, was barren, but Leah, the unloved wife, suddenly began bearing one son after the other.

It should be obvious to us, again, that God hides His greatest surprises in places we least expect them, and we are often caught off guard by how He supplies our needs. It is of great importance to take note of what came forth from these two women.

There was, eventually, some fruit from Rachael. She cried to God in her misery, and he gave her two sons. The first she named Joseph, and we all know his story. Joseph took after his mother, and was beautiful in form and appearance. He went on to become the Prime Minister of Egypt. His younger brother was Benjamin.

Still, from Leah would come so much fruit that it would amaze Jacob. If only he had known it in advance, he might well have treated her differently:

Six of the twelve tribes of Israel were born out of Leah. This means that fifty percent of your successes may well come from that part of your life that you haven't thought much of. God had hidden half of what would make Jacob proud in the wife he had rejected. And you, too, will be surprised to find that much comes forth from areas of your life that you have thought could probably not produce anything.

Never look at circumstances, and never look at outer appearances. Make sure your choices in life are not just fleshly choices. Get the mind of Christ in every decision you make, and fruitfulness awaits you—as it did Jacob (with Leah).

LEAH: MOTHER OF PRAISE

One of the sons born to Leah was named Judah. *Judah* means "praise." How could praise come from a woman in such a sad situation? The highest praise is often born out of hardship and difficulty. Leah had nothing else to do but praise, and she had no one else to praise but God. In her pain, rejection and loneliness, she had to praise God in order to stay positive. Her husband didn't love her, and still she had to carry his child. So, in order to give birth to Judah (praise), she had to learn to praise herself. After all, you can only give what you have.

The highest praise will sometimes come from rejection. The apostles Paul and Silas, when they were jailed in Philippi, praised until the jail opened up. They had all the reason in the world to feel sorry for themselves, but instead, they praised God. Praise opened the prison doors and brought to them deliverance from their circumstances.

Jacob probably thought that praise would come from Rachael, but it was the wife he never wanted from whom praise would come.

I can never forget something I witnessed during my

childhood days in South Africa. We were still in the days of Apartheid, and all the hard labor was done by the blacks of our country. One day I watched as municipal workers got ready to plant a large concrete pole that would carry electricity to the white neighborhoods. The crew was made up of white men, but they found it impossible to lift the heavy pole into place. We had no trucks or mechanical devices to do the job, and so other hands were needed. As usual, blacks were called upon to do the job. I have never forgotten what the black crew did that day to get that heavy pole into place.

> **Leah was rejected by her man, but she knew how to praise God!**

Before attempting to lift the pole, the men gathered a few yards away and began to sing. It was a magical moment. The blacks of South Africa can sing like no one else. They require no instruments because they all harmonize. The sound they made that day, by simply lifting up their voices together, was absolutely heavenly.

These men were doing more than taking a break or entertaining themselves. As they sang, they gathered strength. Then, within a few minutes, they were able to start lifting that pole. As they did so, they kept singing, and as they moved the heavy pole, they continued singing. Their movements almost seemed to be choreographed. They walked that heavy pole up and into the hole prepared for it.

This was not a onetime occurrence. The blacks of South Africa knew a secret. Before tackling any impossible task, they first united in song. In their praise, they found strength that moved them to a higher level and allowed them to do things beyond their natural ability.

Why did the blacks there know this secret so well? The best praise always comes forth out of oppression, and these people were legally excluded from many of life's benefits. Leah was rejected by her man, but she knew how to praise God.

LEAH: ANCESTOR OF KING DAVID

As if Judah were not enough, another incredible man was born of Leah's line. The rejected, looked-down-upon, unwanted Leah went on to become ancestor to the greatest king of Old Testament times. He was none other than David himself, and he, too, was a praiser. As if the praises of Judah were not enough, God brought forth another great worshiper from this unappreciated woman. As a worshiper, David was responsible for many hymns, or psalms. God called him *"a man after His own heart"* (1 Samuel 13:14). When God backs the odd man out, you can know that great things are about to take place, and He backed the unloved and unwanted Leah.

So, never underestimate the seemingly unimportant

things in your life. You never know what God has hiding behind them. Leah was not even in the race to become the chosen one, but when God chooses you, blessings will flow from you that many others would love to have.

LEAH: ANCESTOR OF JESUS HIMSELF

If that were not enough, God went further to honor this woman, pushing her and her descendants so far to the forefront that Rachael, in her wildest dreams, could never hope to catch up. If God takes your side, you can believe that you'll win. When He takes your side, you're in for a promotion.

Not only were six of the twelve tribes of Israel born of Leah, and the praisers, Judah and David, but she received the highest honor possible. One who would be born of her line would provide salvation to the nations, healing for the sick and deliverance for the entire human race. His name, of course, was Jesus. The very Son of the living God was born of that rejected woman. That was the ultimate blessing. What greater thing could possibly be said of her?

It would have been wonderful to be able to ask Jacob, at the end of his life, an important question: "If you had known ahead of time what would come forth from Leah, would you have treated her differently?" Think about it. Never ignore the things that seem unimportant to you.

GOD WAS WATCHING

God was watching how Jacob treated Leah, and nothing can be hidden from His view. If His eye is on the sparrow, then we can be sure that He watches us. God watched Jacob the way Eleazar watched Rebekah, and He's watching you too today.

In the early days of my ministry, I traveled to many nations and visited places that no one else would think of going. I was conscious of the fact that God was watching me, whenever I had to stay in primitive places and eat strange foods for the sake of the Gospel. I can never forget the feeling I had one day as I boarded a plane for India. I knew that God was watching me. He was watching when I traveled through the South American countries and ate foods I was not accustomed to.

There are many easier ministries, and not everyone is interested in the rejected communities of our world. It's much easier for a preacher to preach at home, where there is much more comfort and familiarity. But God is watching, and we must not be guilty of ignoring the places where we may receive no applause for saying something good and no offering to show thankfulness. He is watching, and His reward is with Him.

Like Jacob, you may choose to ignore your Leah, but if you do, you will miss the surprises she can bring. Learn to be faithful in all that you do in life, and you will surely reap eternal rewards.

CHAPTER 12

A GOLDEN NOSE RING AND TWO BRACELETS

So it was, when the camels had finished drinking, that the man took a golden nose ring weighing half a shekel, and two bracelets for her wrists weighing ten shekels of gold, and said, "Whose daughter are you? Tell me, please, is there room in your father's house for us to lodge?"   Genesis 24:22-23

Moreover she said to him, "We have both straw and feed enough, and room to lodge." Then the man bowed down his head and worshiped the LORD.
Genesis 24:25-26

The very moment Rebekah impressed Eleazar, he began to bless her. This *"golden nose ring"* she received as her first gift was as much a part of a women's dress in that era as earrings are today. And that was just the beginning. Next came golden bracelets. But there was still much more to come. Rebekah had no way of knowing it, but when she committed to caring for those pesky camels, she triggered the blessings of Abraham to start flowing into her life.

As we have seen, she was not asked to do this thing. She served willingly and voluntarily out of her heart of goodness. And that was the key.

Don't get a wrong idea from this. Blessings are not something that we need to work for. But if the heart is upright and pure before God, blessings will flow to us—simply because we are moved to strive in all that we do to please God. His desire is to bless us, and He has everything we need. Our obedience will trigger that blessing. Again, these first blessings were just a sign that there was much more to come.

MORE TO COME

When Joshua and Caleb were sent to spy out the land of Canaan, the Bible declares that it *"was the season of the first ripe grapes"* (Numbers 13:20). That means that it was harvest time, the season for blessings. The grapes they carried home with them were just an example of what lay waiting for them in Canaan. There was a lot more where that came from. God doesn't just bless us one time; He is an ever-increasing river of blessings.

When Naomi and Ruth showed up in the land of Boaz, it was *"the beginning of barley harvest"* (Ruth 1:22). The women had made a decision to return to God's land, and they arrived at just the right time. Whenever we serve well, and even when we make a conscious decision to come back to God, He always makes sure it's the right season, the season of gold and silver, the season of blessings.

Ruth, on the advice of her mother-in-law, went to the property of Boaz, a wealthy man of the area, and Boaz, a type of our heavenly Father, invited her in. The result was that the two of them were joined in marriage. From the lineage of Boaz and Ruth came David, one of the most popular kings of the Old Testament, and also from their lineage Jesus was born.

When we are willing to serve, admit, bow down, make adjustments and push aside our own agenda, ideas and ways of doing things, these kinds of blessings will start to flow toward us as well. Many people consider this to be a mere coincidence, but with God, there are no coincidences. With Him, what is happening is always the beginning of something better, the start of a harvest that will never end.

When Rebekah committed to caring for those pesky camels, she triggered the blessings of Abraham to start flowing into her life!

THE FINAL TEST

Rebekah treated Eleazar with such a sweet spirit that he felt emboldened to ask if there might be room for him to stay in her father's house. In this request, he was including those who had accompanied him, as well as the camels. He was now convinced that this was the woman he sought, that she had the heart of a true servant, so he became bold to ask for more. Lodging, in this case, would mean a place to sleep and food to eat for several men and ten large camels. That was no small request. It was a final test.

Without hesitation, Rebekah assured Eleazar that there were enough provisions in her father's house to care for him, his men and their beasts of burden. This shows us several things: One, Rebekah was confident that her father would not be offended by this offer. (It was customary to care for strangers in this way). It shows that her father trusted her. It also reveals that Rebekah was not selfish. She was not worried about keeping what belonged to her family for a time they might need it. She had a generous spirit. It also shows that her willingness to serve went far beyond supplying water. They had other needs, and it was only normal for her to want to meet those needs too. After all, that's what servants do.

Their first absolute necessity had been water, but now that she had learned of a further need, she could not allow that need to go unanswered. Her spirit of serving knew no limits, and she could not permit a need to stand.

Eleazar saw her at the well, so he knew that she could,

at the very least, serve water. Could she do more and would she do more? It didn't take long for these questions to be answered. The moment Rebekah saw the need for more, she offered more. She was willing to serve in any way she needed to.

ENOUGH IS ENOUGH

Today, we think differently. Hadn't she done enough for them already? We have a very commonly used saying: "Enough is enough," and most of us would have considered her first acts "enough." But what is enough? Jesus could have given us salvation and then called that "enough," but He went further and made known to all mankind that He was here to serve man in his fullness—spirit, soul and body.

That being true, why was Eleazar, a type of the Holy Spirit, asking something of Rebekah? He should have been giving to her. It's an important question and one that we need to have answered. One thing is sure: God doesn't need anything from us. This was just another test, and when Rebekah had passed it, the "real" gifts would be revealed.

When God requires something of us, it signals His eagerness to give back to us all that we need ... and more. Rebekah offered Eleazar some straw and feed for his camels, and food and lodging for him and his men, and he gave back to her in the form of gold and silver.

In neither of these cases did Rebekah ask for some reward; it came automatically. Blessings are a release from Heaven, and if we serve well, blessings will fall on us that we have never asked for. Rebekah was not serving with the purpose of getting something in return. We serve, not to get, but to worship. When we worship God, we are brought into a spirit of service. As we adore Him and acknowledge Him and make Him the object toward which we focus all our attention, a deep desire comes to our hearts to do for Him all that we can for as long as we can.

> *When we worship God, we are brought into a spirit of service!*

The offering of the water from your pitcher and the straw from your storeroom can open the gold and silver mines of this world to you. The things Rebekah had to offer were common things, but when we are willing to serve common things, that opens up a flow of the uncommon back to us. With God, we never give gold and receive gold in return or give silver and receive silver in return. We use our simple everyday talents for Him, and He pours out upon us the treasures of Heaven.

LITTLE TO OFFER?

Straw doesn't sound like anything very important at all, and many times what we have to offer may also seem of little value. But if animals need straw to bed down in, then they need straw. To us, straw might not seem very important, but to those who need it, it's invaluable. The thing of little or no value you have in your hand may become something of great, even lifesaving, value to another person.

Animal feed may not seem like much, but when an animal needs it, they can't do without it. The feed she gave those camels at her house that night was to become the fuel they used to convey her back through the desert to her destiny. Imagine that! That seemingly unimportant thing in your hand could be the fuel that carries you to your destiny. If we knew how important the things in our hands are and how significant they can become to our future, we would have a very different attitude toward them.

Sometimes it's the smallest and, seemingly, most insignificant thing that someone has need of. Therefore, what comes out of your pitcher, your pantry and your barn must not be despised. Offering it at the right moment might just activate a flood of blessings upon your life.

Although the water, the straw and the feed were available, they were still not the main issue. It was the spirit of serving that brought the release of the blessings. Nothing would have been known of the pitcher and its contents, the straw, the feed and the lodging, had it not been for the revelation of the spirit of service.

THE WHOLE FAMILY WAS BLESSED

The blessing that Eleazar had brought with him was about to flow further than just to Rebekah. She now ran to tell her family about these things, and they would soon be affected by her blessing. The blessings of God that comes upon you will flow down upon your entire family. They will touch all those around you, in your home, your community, your nation and the world. God has camels packed with blessings, and we need to release them by serving Him. They will bless all. The blessing of God upon my life affects my wife and my daughter as well.

The provision of the straw, the feed and the lodging was a triple act of obedience. Rebekah made Eleazar, his men and his animals comfortable, and only then did he begin to tell her about his true mission and how it would change her life forever.

THE PROPHET WHO TOOK A WIDOW'S LAST CAKE

Rebekah was not the only Bible character to be blessed in return for the offer of food and lodging. A widow, who was called upon to supply a meal and some lodging to the prophet Elisha, was in great need at the time herself. She had only enough flour and oil to prepare one last meal for herself and her son before they succumbed to death (as many already had) due to a severe famine. She must have been surprised when the man of God insisted that she first bake and serve him a cake. Still, she apparently had a servant's heart, for she did what he requested.

That didn't even make sense. Why would a man of God ask a widow and her son to give up their last meal? God had something wonderful in mind. When the woman obeyed, a miracle took place. Her supply of meal and oil was multiplied, and she and her son lived on it through the years of famine. Supplying the basic needs of strangers can sometimes bring an unexpected blessing. The Scriptures declare:

> *Do not forget to entertain strangers, for by so doing some have unwittingly entertained angels.*
>
> Hebrews 13:2

Elisha showed up at the widow's house at what surely seemed to be the most inconvenient moment of her life. But she was not shaken by it. She remained faithful, and she reaped the consequences.

The blessings you have received from the Lord so far are only a down payment, a glimpse of what He has prepared for you. Open your heart to Him, your home, your business, your all, and you'll never be sorry. Heaven's resources are vast and, as God's Spirit finds within you the servant heart, they will be placed at your disposal.

CHAPTER 13

I AM ABRAHAM'S SERVANT

So he said, "I am Abraham's servant."

Genesis 24:34

When the time came for Eleazar to reveal himself to Rebekah and her family, the first thing he told them was the all-important fact—whose servant he was. That said it all. His mission was significant because someone of significance had sent him. The wealth he was about to deliver to them came from a man who, at the time, was considered to be the richest man around. So what made Eleazar important was the person who had sent him. Never be guilty of putting too much emphasis on yourself. Emphasize Him who sent you. Some people have the habit of telling us much more about themselves than they do about Jesus.

EVERYONE KNEW WHAT IT MEANT

"I am the servant of Abraham." That was all Eleazar needed to say. He waited until he was convinced that Rebekah was the chosen one, and then he revealed who

he really was. In that part of the world, everyone knew about Abraham and how blessed he was, so just to say those words, *"I am the servant of Abraham,"* told them the whole story.

Unknowingly, Rebekah and her family had been set up by Eleazar. How well will *you* serve ... when you don't really know whom you're serving?

> **How well will you serve ... when you don't really know whom you're serving?**

Eleazar revealed himself because Rebekah had passed the test. And, because you and I have passed the test of faithfulness, God is about to reveal Himself through the Holy Spirit to us in a remarkable way too. Whatever you do, don't leave your place of service. Stay faithful where God has positioned you. Serve, even though it may not feel good or look good. God is about to reveal to you that you have done well, and a promotion is at hand.

There are thousands of Christian leaders and even many believers who have served well, and I believe that this is the day in which we will all walk right into some incredible blessings. When it happens, we will be overwhelmed and surprised. Get ready for it, for it's surely coming.

YOU ARE ABOUT TO BE LED TO YOUR DESTINY

"I am the servant of Abraham." In other words, Eleazar would lead Rebekah to Abraham and his son. He had received a special commission from his master to perform this function. This was his mission, assigned to him by father Abraham. His role was to do the will of Abraham, and that's exactly what the Holy Spirit is doing in the earth today. Cooperate with Him fully. He has the mind of the Father.

The Spirit of God has one intention. He wants to lead the Church to the place where she can be introduced face-to-face to Jesus. We will then spend eternity in the presence of God. Oh, dear friends, the Holy Spirit is drawing us into a Holy setup, and we will now be introduced to blessings that have been hidden for ages.

In your walk with the Lord, you have done many things, and you have served many people, never knowing whom exactly you were serving and from where they came. Be careful what you do with that one close to you or how you deal with the precious people around you. You never know who their master is or what their particular mission might be.

"I am the servant of Abraham." Eleazar was saying, "You, Rebekah, have served me, but I serve another, one who is greater than I. Your faithfulness to me will now allow me to take you and introduce you to my master."

You and I are destined for a journey. We are chosen for a celebration. We have been handpicked for a choice marriage. Passing the test of service will now bring new revelation to the Church.

THE WEDDING GIFTS REVEALED

At this stage, Rebekah was about to receive the ulti-mate blessing. The initial gifts were good, but on the back of the camels had been carried an even greater blessing. The gold and silver she was about to receive would show the deep intention of the heart of Abraham.

The impending wedding was something that Eleazar knew about, but it was Abraham's idea. The Holy Spirit is here to prepare the Church for a God-idea. It is the idea of the Father in Heaven, and it is intended for those who faithfully serve Him, just as it was His idea to make a way through Jesus for everlasting life.

The gold and silver given now had even more signifi-cance than the previous gifts. They meant much more than being blessed with a nose ring or some bracelets. This second series of gifts were considered to be wedding gifts. When Eleazar was convinced that Rebekah was the one, he did two significant things. First, he revealed who he was, and then he gave Rebekah gifts that were consid-ered to be advance wedding presents.

Wedding gifts are always specific gifts for a specific woman. Eleazar had kept these gifts with him the whole time, but now that he had full clarity of mind about Rebekah's intentions and her ultimate destiny, he gave them to her.

Wedding gifts tell the story. They are gifts that occur

only once in a lifetime, and they signify that a change of name is about to happen. These special gifts were able to convince Rebekah that it was time to depart for her destiny and purpose.

By now, we know that Eleazar is a type of the Holy Spirit and, in the context of this application of truth, it is very significant that he only presented the wedding gifts once he was convinced beyond any reasonable doubt that Rebekah was the actual bride. God sometimes has blessings for us that He withholds for a season until He sees in us the willingness to obey Him and cooperate with His plan for our lives. He tested Abraham first, and once He was convinced that Abraham would obey, He released a blessing over him that was unpredictable, indescribable and incomprehensible.

That day, God had taken the unusual step of swearing to bless Abraham, but this oath was taken only after He had become convinced of who Abraham really was. First, Abraham had to be tested and tried, and only then was the blessing spoken over his life. When God speaks a word, that word can never return void. Therefore God will make absolutely sure of His facts before He releases such a word.

The encounter at the well, with its watering season and the subsequent invitation for Eleazar and all of his entourage to spend the night and be fully provided for, had to happen in the spirit of servanthood before Eleazar could come to a conclusion that would allow him to hand over the wedding gifts. There are gifts that will surely come to us, once our Lord is convinced that we will go all the way with Him. Serve (when you don't know exactly whom you are serving), carry water (when you're not sure exactly for whom you are doing it), and be faithful (without knowing who might be watching you), and you, too, will be blessed.

Once Eleazar revealed the wedding gifts, he fully revealed all his intentions, and he did it in no uncertain language. If Rebekah had entertained any doubts about whether Eleazar really was the servant sent by Abraham, she was convinced once she saw the wedding gifts. Abraham sent gifts no one else could. Soon, she would declare, without reservation, that she wanted to go with this man, and it was the gifts that convinced her.

We are about to see such powerful demonstrations of the Holy Spirit that the world will know, without a shadow of doubt, that the endtime is upon us. We will see God's glory in such a way that all will know that He has other intentions for us than just leaving us where we are. The Holy Spirit is positioning Himself for revealing God's gold and silver, and His gifts will catch the world by surprise.

If we have ever doubted who God is and what He can do, He will now give the Church a new visitation of His glory. As a result, the people of the earth will run after Him, falling in love with Him. The Bride of Christ is to be found on the earth, and I trust that you will be part of her.

IT'S WEDDING-GIFT TIME

Wedding gifts have a certain aroma about them. They announce to the whole world that a man has found his bride and that he wants everyone to know that he is serious about making her his wife. The Church of Jesus Christ is about to enter a season in which He will bestow upon us the wedding gifts. It will be a season of celebration, joy and extreme excitement. The wedding-gift season is the season in which the intentions of the bridegroom are out in the open for everyone to see. The Church of Jesus Christ is a Bride that can expect a revival to soon come upon the earth such as has never been seen in all of human history. Wedding-gift time does not come every day. It is a one-time event, and we need to recognize it when it comes.

> *The Holy Spirit is positioning Himself for revealing God's gold and silver, and His gifts will catch the world by surprise!*

THE BRIDE IS NOT THE FOCUS

On the day of the wedding, it is the bride who always stands out. She is the most important person at the wedding. This season that lies just ahead will be, for the Church, a great time of celebration and feasting. We will be the object of God's attention. But, in this wedding, things are reversed. The Bride is not the focus.

In anticipation of that day, the wedding gifts we are receiving are a clear indication of exactly what our heavenly Bridegroom has in mind. Without Him, there would be no wedding. His gifts indicate more than a seasonal celebration. With God, a wedding is a covenant relationship, and when Abraham sent Eleazar to find a bride, he had a covenant in mind. Today, our God has an eternal celebration in covenant partnership in mind as He woos us by His Spirit.

The greatest gift that God, the Father, could ever give to mankind was His Son Jesus, and He loved us so much that He willingly did that. When He gave His Son, He obviously had eternity in mind. If that did not signify to the human race that God Almighty is serious about His intentions toward us, then what more could He do? He has a wedding planned, and He needs a suitable bride.

As time goes by, we have seen more and more glimpses of God's glory. From time to time, He has revealed Himself in some new way. When Moses saw Him from the back, it changed his life. And throughout the Bible, man was in constant pursuit of this Holy God.

The Shunamite woman was so impressed with a man of God that she asked her husband to spend the money necessary to build a guest room where this man could stay when he was passing through. She wanted the man to spend time in her house, so that she would be blessed. It was God's presence in that man that spawned this desire. The ultimate pleasure of our lives will be to be with Him.

The glory of God is like a great laser beam, shining forth through the night, trying to reach humanity, calling men to join the wedding plans. What is it that has made the Bible such a unique book? Why is it that all of humanity has been striving to discover more about God? What is it about the supernatural that men find so compelling? It's all about the Bridegroom. There is something about Him that is inexplicable. The song writer said it well: "Jesus, there's just something about that name," and you and I are destined to be joined to Him for all eternity.

Ultimately, God's Spirit will convince many men and women to say yes for their ride to destiny. How about you? Let your journey begin today on the back of your camel. The thing that could have bitten you will turn and become the vehicle that carries you to your greatest moment in life. Rebekah, once she saw those wedding gifts, gave the journey a yes. *"I will go,"* she said. Our Lord is waiting to hear those words from each of us.

CHAPTER 14

I WILL GO

Then they called Rebekah and said to her, "Will you go with this man?" And she said, "I will go."

Genesis 24:58

What happened with Rebekah could rightly be called The Great Adventure, but what triggers such a great adventure is just as important. The trigger, in Rebekah's case, was her willing servant's heart. The test of her life involved some camels, and that brings us back to those smelly beasts. There is so much about the life of Rebekah on which we could have focused this book, but what was key to it all was how she treated those camels. If the camels had not been served, the blessing would never have come to her.

Rebekah could have served Eleazar well, but if she had neglected the camels, she would have missed her covenant bond with Isaac. Those seemingly unimportant camels were the hiding place for her blessing. As we have seen, she could have easily ignored them (and refused to serve them), and who would have blamed her? If she had done that, Eleazar would have gone back home empty-handed or sought a bride elsewhere, and Rebekah would never have even known that she had missed out on her great destiny. By not being faithful in the seemingly mundane things of life, we often miss great opportunities, and we don't even know we've had opportunities to miss.

Serving well means being faithful in areas the majority of people neglect. Out of the many women at that well, only one offered to serve the camels. To serve well is to help those who are in need when others have not even recognized the need. To serve well is to serve the master, as well as all that is his. Rebekah saw the camels, recognized their need and accepted it as her own responsibility. That act won her Isaac's hand in marriage.

Many people are guilty of not even taking care of their own responsibilities, much less accepting responsibility for others. It was not difficult to see that Eleazar had a need, but Rebekah saw beyond his need, to the need of the camels, and then she made that problem her own. A true servant sees needs before they can be announced. This is wise, for seemingly unimportant things, situations, conditions or even people often carry gifts to us from the throne room of God, and we must be sensitive toward the Holy Spirit to understand who and what we are dealing with at all times.

Eleazar did not feel the need to make a public announcement about the thirst of his camels, and it was taken care of before he could even mention it. That's the type of servant we desperately need in the Church today. True servants are concerned about more than their own needs. They serve the needs of others as if they were their own.

Oh friend, the thing you feel like ignoring in life is the very thing you need to serve. The area that you see as a challenge to be avoided is the challenge you need to accept. Then, go one step further. Prepare yourself for a surprise waiting at the well of your daily responsibilities. In the middle of your daily rush of busyness, you will find an opportunity to serve. Serve well, as you never know where that act of service might take you.

> *Serving well means being faithful in areas the majority of people neglect!*

Most people, before committing to anything today, want to know what they can get out of it. "What's in it for me?" A servant never sees a need in that way. He's not seeking what he can get *out of it,* but what he can give others *through it.*

Jesus did not come to this earth for what He could get out of the experience. He knew that what awaited Him, as a reward for His act of service, was pain and humiliation. Still, He served well, so that we can have the eternal benefits. It was the benefits of His service that paid the price for our salvation, our healing and our deliverance.

A servant is not constantly thinking of himself; he is thinking of those whom he serves. The act of service is part of his lifestyle.

Beloved, let us look past the challenges, the obstacles, the frustrations and who will receive the glory, and let us be found faithful at our wells of responsibility. Serve all that come your way, as you never know the next setup by the Holy Spirit that could take you to your purpose in life and fulfill your destiny. Get the pitchers, and let us pour water for those who are thirsty. Come now, for it is time to *Feed the Camels.*

– NOTES –

– NOTES –

Other ministry resources from André van Zyl:

Single CD Messages

- Married to Leah
- Trophies of Christ's Victory
- The Presence of God
- The Breath of God
- Seventh Day Revelation
- From this Day Forward
- I Swear I Will Bless You
- Breaking the Flask
- God to Pharoah
- The Sound of Rain
- Divine Protection
- Passing Your Breaking Point
- Unwrap Resurrection Power
- Barley in My Tjarley
- Thronging or Touching
- Strengthen Yourself in the Lord
- Three Seasons of a Prophetic Word
- Fruitfulness in the Land of My Affliction
- A Divine Catch
- Spy Out Your Destiny
- Abundance at Your Door
- Bow and Arrows—Generation to Generation
- You!
- Go After it
- Revive! The Wagons Are Here

- Break Loose from Old Bondage's and Conditions
- The DNA of the Bread Changed
- I Came to My Senses
- Healing, Outside the Comfort Zone
- It's in the House
- The Word is Out—TOMORROW

Double CD Messages

- Feed the Camels
- Building a Room for the Holy Spirit
- Announce Your Freedom

Other Books by André van Zyl

- Destined for the Palace
- What do You See?

For more products and ordering information,
call: (770) 271-4421
email: gnninfo@aol.com
or log on to the ministry website: http://www.gnni.org/

New CDs and books will become available!

Good News to the Nations

You may communicate with the author at the
following address:

André and Naomi van Zyl
Good News to the Nations, Inc.
2463 Hamilton Mill Pkwy.,
Suite 280-308
Dacula, GA 30019

Telephone: (770)271-4421
Email: gnninfo@aol.com
www.gnni.org